Baffled By Bitcoin

A Simple Guide To The Money Of Tomorrow

Bit Noi

Copyright © 2020 Bit Noi
All rights reserved.

CONTENTS

Foreword 5
1. Introduction 8
2. What 16
Genesis 18
The Double-Spend Problem 21
Back To Basics 24
Satoshi Nakamoto 27
The Story So Far 34
The What Chapter Summary 39
3. How 40
Blockchain 42
Nodes 46
Miners 48
Hash Rate 51
Difficulty 53
The Halving 55
The Mining Ecosystem 57
Proof of Work (POW) vs Proof of Stake (POS) 60

Forks 63
The Almighty 51% 65
Wallets 68
Exchanges 71
The Lightning Network 73
The How Chapter Summary 75
4. Why 77
Scarcity 79
What is Money? 85
Money Problems 89
The Gold Standard 93
Stock-to-Flow 98
The Fiat Era 102
The Bitcoin Era? 114
Bitcoin as a Store of Value 123
Bitcoin in the Developing World 128
Deflation by Design 132
The Why Chapter Summary 141
5. Why Not 143
Fact or Fiction? 145
6. Conclusion 162
Block by Block 164
The Future 167
7. Additional Resources 170
8. Glossary 172
9. Thank You 178

Foreword

If you're reading this line, I'd like to congratulate you. You have taken the first step in discovering the exciting new world of Bitcoin. Whatever your motivations for reading this book, you are about to learn some amazing stuff. You may have accepted that you are indeed Baffled by Bitcoin, which is more than can be said for many newbies who enter the space.

A position of *conscious incompetence* is a great place to start because you open yourself up to *learn* things. I certainly wish when I first got into the "crypto" world I was a bit more consciously incompetent as it probably would have saved me many painful and expensive mistakes.

I first discovered Bitcoin in late 2017, like many other people, just as it was surging towards its all-time high prices. I came at it from an investment perspective as I had a little bit of money to invest and I didn't fancy buying stocks which had been rising almost non-stop for around 7 years. Initially, I had some success buying various cryptocurrencies, but, failing to recognize the impending crash, all those gains soon evaporated and I was left with some heavy losses. I think it's fair to say I've probably fallen into every trap in the book and made every mistake along the way but something stuck with me.

I felt compelled to learn more. I couldn't quite accept that this could just be a bubble. Working as a finance professional, I started digging into Bitcoin's economic principles and the fundamentals that give it its value. What I discovered is quite shocking. But whilst it was shocking, simultaneously the pennies were dropping in my mind. I urge you to persevere, even if some things don't make sense at first, to read and reread this book and others that are available on the subject until that penny drops for you.

This book is the product of many hours spent toiling by a normal guy. I'm not some OG millionaire that has been into Bitcoin since the beginning, I'm not one of the developers, I'm not the owner of a cryptocurrency exchange and unfortunately, I'm not William Shakespeare. I'm just a normal person that has made a lot of mistakes and learned a huge amount. I felt compelled to write this book to help people avoid making those same mistakes and to educate people about something that could have a massive impact on our lives.

And no, Bit Noi is not my real name. It is a pseudonym. I simply value my privacy too much to write without a pen name.

So without further ado, I invite you to join me as we enter the Bitcoin rabbit hole...

Disclaimer: The ideas and concepts in this book are written purely for educational purposes. Nothing written in this book is intended or should be construed as financial or investment advice.

1.

Introduction

It's 6 a.m. The alarm goes off. A flailing arm batters it into snooze. 10 minutes later, it's going again. Rubbing the sleep from his eyes, Jeff drags himself out of bed. "Maybe that last episode of Stranger Things wasn't such a great idea", he thinks. Jeff has been working long hours in his office job and struggles to find much free time for his own leisure activities.

Outside it is a dreary morning in the Big Apple. The rain is holding off for now but the air smells damp and it is decidedly autumnal. A smog sits above the city, generated by the bumper to bumper gridlock forming as rush hour gets started. There is a cacophony of horns, engines, and the distant rumble of the subway. Just another day.

Jeff takes a shower and gets dressed for work. His shirt is a little threadbare on the collar and cuffs, but it should pass normal inspection. Besides, renting in New York is an expensive business and Jeff seldomly has any spare cash that he can justify spending on work clothes.

He flicks on the television whilst eating his toast. "The economy is booming!" the talking heads proclaim, as they report record gains in the stock markets. It doesn't feel like that to Jeff. He hasn't had a meaningful pay rise in years, yet his rent seems to increase every 12 months without fail. He'd like to own his own home but with New York real estate prices what they are he can forget about that ambition.

Jeff takes a deep breath and exits his flat. "Another day, another dollar", he thinks. As he makes his way to the subway he weaves past several rough sleepers, "I'm sure there never used to be this many homeless people around here" he thinks to himself, "they must have been moved on from somewhere." Meanwhile, up ahead in the traffic he hears the deep roar of a sports car, sprinting from one red light to the next. It looks like a Lamborghini. "Must be on their way to Wall Street", Jeff thinks to himself.

Jeff can't make it to the subway without passing the usual plethora of coffee chains. On autopilot, he heads in to pick up his usual morning brew. "Would you like to try our new blend sourced directly from the deepest rainforests of Indonesia?" an enthusiastic clerk asks. "Sure, why not." Jeff responds, more out of surprise than anything else. "Great, that'll be $5." Jeff winces and remembers when a cup of coffee would cost less than $2. He begrudgingly hands over a $5 bill and sets off on his way, single-use plastic cup in hand.

Jeff spends the next eleven hours or so commuting to the office, working in a small cubicle with little natural light and commuting home again. He had arranged to meet up with some friends this evening but he's exhausted and short of cash. He already has a large credit card bill that needs paying off with this month's paycheck. Reluctantly he decides to cancel his friends and settles down for another night of Netflix and chilling, by himself.

He'd like to start a family one day but at the moment he simply doesn't have the energy for dating. "Someone to share the bills with would be quite handy though", he thinks as he smiles to himself.

Jeff switches on the television. The talking heads are still going. He doesn't understand much of what they are talking about but they are the experts after all. He trusts that if they are saying things are better than ever before, they must be. Mustn't they? Jeff can't quite put his finger on it but he goes to bed that night wondering, are things really better than ever? It doesn't seem that way in the *real* world. Weary from the daily grind, it's not long before Jeff drifts off and the cycle starts all over again the next day.

No, you haven't picked up the wrong book. This is a book about Bitcoin, but it's about economics just as much. You see, Jeff is like millions of others who are starting to question what is *really* going on in our global economy. While we're told things have never been better, and shown charts of the stock markets to prove it, something simply doesn't feel right for the majority of people.

Certain people are able to amass incredible wealth, we have more billionaires than ever before, yet that seems to be at the expense of millions of others. For every billionaire hotshot, there are now thousands of people needing to use food banks just to feed their families. Inequality is rife. Is this really how our economies should be functioning?

That's where Bitcoin comes in. Bitcoin has the potential to change this. That's not to say it will, but it *could.* This is why we talk about the Bitcoin "rabbit hole". Once you go in, there's no going back.

* * *

"If you don't believe it or don't get it, I don't have the time to try to convince you, sorry."

\- *Satoshi Nakamoto*

This book isn't intended to convince you one way or another about Bitcoin. It is simply a compilation of truths, a collection of information that will enable you to make your own informed decisions. Bitcoin remains a mystery to many people so you are already way ahead of the game just by showing enough curiosity to read up on it.

While the concept of Bitcoin is quite a simple one, a form of digital cash, its application in the real world is anything but simple. It exists in a complex economic world of our own creation and finds itself as the pioneer of an exciting new technology. It is something that could change the world, perhaps.

Exactly how Bitcoin's future plays out remains to be

seen, we are in unprecedented times both socially and economically as the globe grapples with an ongoing pandemic. This book doesn't have all the answers. No book does. What this book does offer is a simple explanation of all aspects of "magic internet money" as Bitcoin is sometimes referred.

This name may sound facetious but to many people, that's exactly what it is. It functions like money, it exists online, and it has a growing army of enthusiasts who proclaim it to be the next big thing, so it must be magic? Understandably the majority of normal folk are left scratching their head over exactly what all the fuss is about.

Money is not a subject of interest for most people. Yes, many of us would like a bit more of it, but money itself, its purpose, its functions, its origins, are not topics that often come up in conversation among anyone outside of financial occupations. The main reason for this is the apparent complexity of our economies. Most people simply don't understand all the technical jargon, figures, and indicators that we are subjected to by those "in the know". The economy is a very complicated thing, so best left to the experts, right?

It is perhaps no surprise then, that often people are first drawn into Bitcoin as a means of making a bit more money, an investment. Bitcoin has been through numerous bubbles that, timed right, can yield enormous returns. But, timed badly, it can also yield enormous losses. Whatever your purpose for getting into Bitcoin, a solid understanding of the cryptocurrency is essential.

While some see it purely as a speculative instrument,

it goes much deeper than that. It is part cutting-edge new technology, part experimental new currency, part empowering custodian, and part freedom fighter. Looking at just one element doesn't give you the full picture.

Of course, all that probably doesn't mean much to you right now, but it will. This book is designed to take you on a magical mystery tour of all things Bitcoin, split simply into the *What, How, Why,* and *Why Not.*

The *What* is exactly that. The basics. A simple explanation of what Bitcoin is, what it does, how you use it, and so on. We'll also delve into the mystery of Bitcoin's early days and its mysterious creator, while summarizing a potted history of the cryptocurrency and some of the major events that have shaped it during its life thus far.

If you have done any prior reading about Bitcoin some of these elements will be familiar to you, but this book is designed to give a complete beginner the essential foundations to go on and understand the many other aspects of Bitcoin.

A big part of that is the *How*. Bitcoin is primarily a technology invention so there's a lot of techy elements to understand. But don't worry if you are not technically minded, they are broken down into manageable chunks and explained in layman's terms to slowly build up layer upon layer of knowledge.

You may think the technology isn't such an important aspect to understand. After all, you can manage with the internet just fine and you may not have read any books about that. This viewpoint is entirely understandable and it is true that to use bitcoin you don't need to know exactly how it works, as long as you know enough to be able to operate with it. But the technology is so intrinsically linked to Bitcoin's modus operandi that it is strongly encouraged that you take the time to digest this chapter carefully as it fills many of the gaps in the big picture.

Equipped with the knowledge of what Bitcoin is and how it works, you are ready to tackle the *Why*. This is where we really go deeper into the rabbit hole and by far the most important chapter in this book. Understanding the motivations for creating Bitcoin involves first gaining an understanding of what we consider money to be. What we think sound money should look like. This may be something you have never even considered, as we have precious little choice over what money we would like to use.

Evaluating money is a real eye-opener and you will find yourself re-reading certain sections in this chapter in disbelief. Some of the truths uncovered seem simply unfathomable. It is certainly a complex area where there are huge amounts of misinformation and misdirection in the mainstream media. Bitcoin is bringing these problems with our current financial system into the light.

While Bitcoin has the potential to perhaps solve some of our economic problems, it is by no means perfect. You may have heard or read negative stories about it in the press. In the *Why Not* we look at some of the most prevalent criticisms of Bitcoin and give a balanced account of their merits.

It seems that almost everyone these days has something to say about Bitcoin, so how do you know who to trust and whether they are talking any sense? Some of the most common soundbites you'll hear are addressed and the most misleading myths debunked.

As with all of the chapters within this book, you can dive much much deeper into any aspect of Bitcoin and there is a wealth of information online. You can even find online virtually all the early forum posts from those that were involved right from the very beginning. Bitcoin is growing both in popularity and adoption, and every day more and more excellent educational content is appearing online.

It is still a relatively new technology and is developing and changing before our very eyes, interacting with its environment in new ways all the time as more people start to discover and use it. It is quite fascinating to see this play out in real-time and something that you really should be paying attention to. You could say a quiet revolution has begun.

2. What

"I think the internet is going to be one of the major forces for reducing the role of government. The one thing that's missing but that will soon be developed, is a reliable e-cash."

- *Milton Friedman, economist who received the 1976 Nobel Memorial Prize in Economic Sciences*

If you've picked up this book you must be pretty curious, or just downright confused as to what on Earth this Bitcoin thing is.

Let's start with the basics. Bitcoin is a cryptocurrency, a form of money that exists only digitally. This definition is deceptively simple. The rabbit hole goes much deeper than this.

Bitcoin is something the world has never seen before. A revolutionary new technology that has the potential to change our lives by an order of magnitude akin to the creation of the internet. Still in its reasonably early days, it is growing in adoption all the time and slowly starting to establish itself as a genuine candidate to be the future of money.

Like all new technologies, it certainly takes more than a little thought to get your head around. Trying to familiarize ourselves with something that we cannot easily compare to anything that already exists is a difficult task. But it can be done. And it is worth doing.

To set us on our way to understanding what Bitcoin is, and what it does, let's start at the very beginning.

Genesis

On 18 August 2008, the domain name "bitcoin.org" was registered. A few months later on 31 October, a link to a whitepaper titled *"Bitcoin: A Peer-to-Peer Electronic Cash System"* was posted on a cryptography mailing list.

On 3rd January 2009 the Bitcoin network was born, as the genesis block (block 0) was created. What does this actually mean? It means the first computer ever to run the Bitcoin network had been switched on.

Embedded within the genesis block was the headline from UK newspaper the Times that day:

"The Times 03/Jan/2009 Chancellor on brink of second bailout for banks"

Bitcoin had been born in the midst of one of the worst financial crises in years.

Within a week the code to run Bitcoin had been made publicly available online as an open-source protocol. Others started downloading the software and running Bitcoin, and on 12 January 2009 the first-ever bitcoin transfer was made for 10 bitcoin.

The Bitcoin whitepaper outlines the functions and purpose of the Bitcoin network. Far from being a voluminous mammoth text that you might expect, the whitepaper is only 9 pages long including references. It is highly recommended you read this if you want to understand Bitcoin further, even if much of it may not make sense at first.

The abstract set out quite simply what the Bitcoin network set out to achieve:

> *"A purely peer-to-peer version of electronic cash would allow online payments to be sent directly from one party to another without going through a financial institution"*

This is something you may never have even thought about. After all, it seems so easy to send money online through internet banking. But this is a significant difference between the online and offline world. Offline, you can choose to transact in cash. Yes, you still need a bank to ultimately issue that cash but you can make transactions directly with another person without the involvement of a third party. Before Bitcoin, that was simply not possible to do online.

No form of "digital cash" existed. This is quite strange when you consider just how much e-commerce had boomed in the 2000s. Perhaps then, it was inevitable that some form of digital cash would eventually be developed, and it was Bitcoin that got there first.

The simplest way to think about bitcoin is as a digital dollar that can be sent from any individual to another directly, in the same way you would send an email.

But what exactly is a bitcoin? By definition, it is a chain of electronic signatures. For every transaction, the owner of the coin digitally signs a hash of the previous transaction before adding the public key of the next owner to the end of the coin. This is all a form of cryptography, hence the term "cryptocurrency", which is also used in other areas of technology such as email and instant messaging. If your instant messaging app offers encrypted messages this is the same form of technology at work.

Don't worry if the technicalities don't make sense right now, as we'll talk about that in more detail in the *How* chapter.

In essence, then, a bitcoin is a piece of computer code that is verified through encryption. The question is, if encryption was already in use for email and other functions, why did it take so long to develop digital cash?

The Double-Spend Problem

The main reason digital cash has taken so long to be developed is that digital items are so easily copied. If you have a document on your computer you can create another copy at the touch of a button. You can send a copy of the same document to anyone who has an email address, even to thousands of people at the same time. Or you may choose to upload that document to a web page where potentially millions of people might download it.

Obviously then, the idea of digital cash that you store on your computer like a PDF or an MP3 file would never work. Quite soon the supply of any such type of money would skyrocket as everyone furiously hit copy and paste and as a result, it would be worthless. Therefore, for digital cash, normal types of computer files simply don't work.

To put this more formally, you have what is known as the double-spend problem. When making a transaction, how does the recipient know that the digital cash has not already been used once or even many times before? With physical cash, we don't have this problem as the physical note is handed over at the point of purchase. While a determined counterfeiter could make copies of physical cash, this is quite difficult to do and realistically most people would not risk doing so due to the risk of prosecution.

The way around the double-spend problem with digital cash is to keep a digital ledger of all transactions. If every transaction is recorded in a ledger, whoever has access to that ledger can verify that each dollar is only being spent once. So long as that ledger is maintained and kept up-to-date any attempted double-spending can be eliminated.

This is how traditional online banking does work. Banks keep their own ledgers and can ensure that no dollar is accounted for twice anywhere in the system. But what if whoever maintained that ledger had nefarious intentions? What's to stop them adding some new digital dollars to their balance on the ledger? Absolutely nothing. In reality, laws and regulations are in place that should prevent this from happening but technologically there is nothing to stop them. They are the trusted third party, the middleman of online transactions, and a single point of failure in the system should they elect to breach that trust.

This is a problem when it comes to creating digital cash. But fortunately, there is a simple solution. If the ledger is made public to everyone, and everyone keeps a copy *themselves,* then everyone can verify that the transactions being posted to the ledger are valid. If you try to spend digital cash you don't have then your transaction will be refused as everyone can see that you don't have the cash you're trying to spend. If you try to create new digital cash from thin air, again you'll be reprimanded as everyone else can see that you are creating fictitious entries in the ledger. With this method so long as the majority of participants agree on what is the valid ledger, any attempted deviations can be dismissed.

In essence, this is exactly how Bitcoin works. Every computer that connects to the Bitcoin network downloads a record of every transaction ever made. As new transactions are made, provided a majority of network participants agree they are valid transactions, they are then added to the ledger and distributed to all participants. This is all done automatically by computers connected to the network known as miners.

This technology underpinning the Bitcoin network is known as blockchain, as blocks of transactions are chained together into the blockchain which becomes the digital ledger. Many cryptocurrencies have been built using blockchain technology but Bitcoin was the first to ever gain any sort of mainstream traction, and is by far the biggest in terms of value.

As the ledger is maintained on hundreds or thousands of different computers connected to the network, the network is said to be decentralized, meaning there is no central control and no single point of failure. Even if a large number of computers were to be disconnected, the others in the network can continue maintaining the ledger without issue. It is also a trustless network, as every participant can verify the ledger for themselves, therefore no-one is left having to trust that a third-party has maintained it honestly.

While this explanation may sound simple, a digital solution to the double-spend problem eluded computer scientists for many years until the Bitcoin whitepaper was published by Bitcoin's elusive creator, Satoshi Nakamoto, in 2008.

Back To Basics

Before we get too deep in the details, you are probably wondering what some of all this technical speak actually means. Let's take a step back and summarize simply what Bitcoin is and how you can actually use it.

A bitcoin is a unit of digital cash, as outlined above, denoted by the symbol as seen in orange on the cover of this book. Each bitcoin can be split into 100 million smaller chunks known as sats, named after Satoshi Nakamoto. This is the equivalent of a dollar being split into 100 cents, except rather than using 2 decimal places, each bitcoin can be split down to 8 decimal places. So one sat is expressed as 0.00000001 bitcoin. Sometimes bitcoin is shortened to BTC.

When we talk about bitcoin, we can be referring to a digital coin, or the word Bitcoin can also be used to describe the Bitcoin network. The network is a series of thousands of computers that maintain the digital ledger of transactions. Every bitcoin transaction ever made is on the ledger, and every computer connected to the network has a complete copy of them.

New bitcoin are generated by computers on the network known as miners. The miners solve cryptography puzzles and every time a solution is found a new block is added to the ledger. The miner's reward for solving the puzzle is a set amount of new bitcoin. These block rewards reduce over time and by the year 2140 all bitcoin will have been mined. The total number of bitcoin in circulation at this point will be just under 21 million. At the time of writing around 18 million of these have already been mined.

The miners who receive new bitcoin are free to keep them or sell them on exchanges, websites that enable users to buy and sell bitcoin between US dollars and other currencies. In the very early days, the only way you could get bitcoin would be to mine them, however nowadays with the wide range of exchanges available it is very easy to buy them with dollars or many other currencies.

If you want to store some bitcoin you need a wallet, just like you'd keep cash in your wallet in real life. Wallets can be online or offline but all will have a public key and a private key. To receive bitcoin you simply need to give the sender an address generated from the public key, this acts much like your bank account details. However, to send bitcoin out of your wallet you need the private key, it is therefore vital that this key is kept, well, private! It shouldn't be shared otherwise you run the risk of your bitcoin being stolen. These keys take the form of a 256-bit number, basically a string of 64 characters between A-Z and 0-9.

Bitcoin cannot be destroyed as they are always accounted for on the digital ledger that is maintained by the network. However, they can be lost, or rather the private keys can be lost. Losing your private keys means that those bitcoin can no longer be moved, they will remain in the same wallet forevermore until those keys are found. It is estimated that up to 20% of all bitcoin are already lost as investors lost interest over time and failed to securely look after their keys, not realizing how valuable bitcoin would become.

Bitcoin have value because there is demand for them. They are a censorship-resistant tool to transfer wealth between individuals. This is incredibly powerful. While the early days saw incredibly volatile swings in price, if adoption continues to grow the value of bitcoin should start to plateau and the volatility should eventually subside.

Satoshi Nakamoto

So who came up with this ingenious solution to the double-spend problem? A mysterious character known only as Satoshi Nakamoto. Exactly who Satoshi is, no-one knows for sure. Or if they do, they're keeping it pretty quiet.

Satoshi's first post online of any sort was the publication of the Bitcoin whitepaper in October 2008. Following that they were active in sending emails and making many online forum posts as the Bitcoin network was launched and the code developed further. Then suddenly in 2011, they left the project and vanished from the cryptocurrency space.

So who was Satoshi, and why did they decide to leave the project just as Bitcoin was starting to gain some traction?

There are numerous theories as to the identity of the real Satoshi, and many people have claimed to be Satoshi but as of yet, no one person has been able to prove definitively that they are indeed Satoshi. Given that they went to great lengths to protect their real identity and then left the Bitcoin project, it seems strange that they would now step forward and reveal themselves to the world, therefore any such claims are best viewed with skepticism.

Besides, there is a very simple way that the real Satoshi could prove their identity. In the very early days of Bitcoin, Satoshi mined a tremendous number of coins. In fact, in wallets associated with Satoshi, there are around *one million bitcoin*. At the 2017 peak, they would have been worth $20 billion, putting Satoshi among the 100 richest people on Earth. These bitcoin have never moved.

If the real Satoshi wanted to prove their identity all they would have to do is simply transfer one bitcoin or even one sat out of these wallets. The fact that they have never moved suggests Satoshi has no desire to spend them or may even mean that Satoshi is no longer alive.

Do a little bit of digging, however, and you will come across some clues as to who may have been behind the pseudonym. Cryptography was a hot topic at the time among a group known as the cypherpunks, who were concerned about the issue of privacy in the new digital world the internet had birthed. The cypherpunk ranks included those such as Julian Assange, whose name you may recognize from its association with the Wikileaks website that caused great controversy in the late 2000s and early 2010s.

In fact, at one point Satoshi briefly talked Assange out of using bitcoin to raise donations for Wikileaks, fearing that it had "kicked the hornet's nest" in bringing unwanted government attention on Bitcoin whilst it was still in its infancy. As it happened, shortly after Satoshi disappeared, Wikileaks did launch a bitcoin donations address and used it to raise tens of millions of dollars with governments seemingly powerless to intervene.

Many of the cypherpunks had been experimenting with digital cash through projects such as B-Money,

Hashcash, and Bit Gold, some of which are even referenced in the Bitcoin whitepaper. When reading in Bitcoin circles you will come across many names closely associated with the technology, some of whom continue to work on and develop Bitcoin as part of its core development team.

However, some stand out and are worth a special mention.

Hal Finney

Hal Finney was a computer scientist based in California. He was heavily involved in cryptography and helped develop the technology behind proof-of-work systems that would form a key part of the Bitcoin protocol. He was also one of the cypherpunks and had strong ideals around privacy and freedom.

Hal was active on the forums around the time Satoshi started posting about Bitcoin and while most people were skeptical about Bitcoin and whether it could actually work, he was positive about the project from the get-go. In fact, just one week after the genesis block was created in January 2009, Hal posted this online:

> *"As an amusing thought experiment, imagine that Bitcoin is successful and becomes the dominant payment system in use throughout the world. Then the total value of the currency should be equal to the total value of all the wealth in the world. Current estimates of total worldwide household wealth that I have found range from $100 trillion to $300 trillion. With 20 million coins, that gives*

each coin a value of about $10 million."

Given that at the time Bitcoin was a fledgling software project that no-one was using, that is quite a bold prediction and shows an awful lot of faith from someone that has just come across the project!

Hal Finney was also present at several of Bitcoin's key milestones. He is considered to be the first person other than Satoshi to run Bitcoin, simply tweeting on 11th January 2009; "Running bitcoin". He was also the recipient of the first-ever bitcoin transaction of 10 bitcoin.

Unfortunately, Hal was diagnosed with amyotrophic lateral sclerosis (ALS) in 2009 and died from complications related to the illness in 2014. When questioned during his lifetime about being Satoshi he always denied any involvement, but could it be that he moved away from the project as a result of his debilitating illness to spend more time with his family? We will never know, but certainly, Hal remains the most likely Satoshi in many people's eyes.

Nick Szabo

Nick Szabo was another cypherpunk that was very interested in creating digital cash. He had even published a blog post about his proposal, Bit Gold, as far back as 2005. Nick's post details the problems of inflation and relying on third-party involvement for financial transactions; some of the exact problems that Bitcoin could potentially solve.

Interestingly, Nick's Bit Gold project is not referenced in the Bitcoin whitepaper even though some other early digital cash projects such as B-Money and Hashcash are. Satoshi even confirmed in later blog posts that Bitcoin was modeled on Bit Gold, so this omission from the whitepaper doesn't make a lot of sense. Furthermore, there is no known email correspondence between Nick and Satoshi, while other developers such as Hal Finney communicated regularly with Satoshi and made their correspondence publicly available.

It is possible Nick and Satoshi were not aware of each other's projects but that would make for a remarkable coincidence given their similarity in name and form, and Satoshi's later confirmation of Bit Gold being the model for Bitcoin. Also, it would seem that Nick just abandoned Bit Gold once Bitcoin came along, which is quite strange if the two were completely separate projects. Even stranger, he showed no interest in becoming involved with Bitcoin. For a man with such a strong interest in this area, to sit back and do nothing at all at this time does seem very odd!

While he would regularly write blog posts, Bitcoin did not get a mention until May 2009, a full 4 months after the first block was mined. The frequency of Nick's blog posts also dramatically reduced following the launch, and the date on his 2005 Bit Gold blog post mysteriously changed to 2008, to post-date the Bitcoin whitepaper. Nick did not start writing about Bitcoin in detail until 2011, just after Satoshi disappeared.

And finally, there's the Freudian slip. In a 2017 interview Nick said:

"I'd definitely go for a second layer, I mean, I designed Bitcoi ... gold with two layers."

A slip of the tongue, or the words of the real Satoshi?

Dorian Nakamoto

One face you may have seen pop up all over the internet is that of Dorian Nakamoto. A Japanese-American retired physicist who found himself at the center of a media storm in 2014 after a journalist published an article supposedly revealing the identity of the real Satoshi.

When questioned about Bitcoin, Dorian had responded "I am no longer involved in that and I cannot discuss it." That was perhaps the worst thing he could have said and given his well-educated background and career in physics, the media ran with the story. He would later clarify his comments, and state that he believed he was being asked about his work on classified projects during his career.

It is generally accepted that Dorian is not the real Satoshi, nor even involved with Bitcoin at all. On seeing the story, the Bitcoin community was outraged at the invasion of privacy of Dorian, and a fundraising page was set up to compensate him, raising 102 bitcoin!

However, the story doesn't end there. What was Dorian's full name? Dorian Prentice Satoshi Nakamoto.

And where did he live? Just a few blocks away from Hal Finney. Now there's a coincidence.

In reality, we will probably never know exactly who the real Satoshi is, or was, and it could well have been more than one person working together. The fact of the matter is, Bitcoin is a decentralized system by design, so it's probably best that the true identity of Satoshi Nakamoto remains one of the world's great mysteries.

The Story So Far

From its humble beginnings, Bitcoin has grown into a phenomenon that is now known about by millions of people around the globe, to the extent that you are now reading this book. So how has Bitcoin become so popular and how has it managed to avoid all the pitfalls along the way that threatened to derail it?

When Bitcoin was first developed by Satoshi it initially started to catch on among cypherpunks and computer scientists interested in cryptography. In the early days Bitcoin was just a technological experiment, no-one really knew whether the technology would actually work, or whether it could grow to any sort of usable size.

While bitcoins are effectively digital cash, Bitcoin as a whole is basically just a network. A network of separate computers all working together in a decentralized manner to maintain the digital ledger of transactions. Like any network, this network could be susceptible to attack, or errors in its code which could cause it to malfunction or even go down altogether. Unlike traditional networks, there is no single point of failure as there is no central control, so the larger the network grows, in theory, the stronger it becomes.

In the early days, Satoshi and other developers experimented with the code and continued to iron out problems. Of which there were a few. One notable example became known as the "Value Overflow incident", where 184 billion bitcoin were inadvertently created instead of the usual 50 that were awarded for mining a block.

This was noticed pretty quickly and within 5 hours of its discovery the code had been corrected and the billions of extra bitcoin removed from the ledger.

Over time this team of developers grew and took over the reins once Satoshi disappeared. Nowadays there exists a Bitcoin Foundation which works to promote the continued development and uptake of the cryptocurrency. Due to Bitcoin's open-source nature, anyone can join developer communities and develop code for improvements to the protocol. Understandably, there is a thorough review process in place before any updates to the code are made.

The first commercial transaction completed with bitcoin, albeit indirectly, was the purchase of two Papa John's pizzas in 2010, for 10,000 bitcoin. Also in 2010, the first bitcoin exchanges started appearing online. An exchange is just a website that allows users to buy or sell bitcoin with US dollars or other currencies.

Over the ensuing years, bitcoin would grow in adoption but that adoption would primarily come from criminals and black markets. As you can imagine, criminals can find it difficult to move money around as the banks can easily close down their accounts or freeze their assets. With bitcoin, rightly or wrongly, there were no such restrictions.

This is a big part of the reason that bitcoin had such a tainted reputation in its early days and that stigma continues to this day. Of course, in reality, criminals use all sorts of currencies and technologies but that doesn't mean they're all bad!

With only a limited number of bitcoin in circulation and more people becoming interested in using the cryptocurrency, the price of a bitcoin was subject to wild fluctuations. In 2011 the bitcoin price started at 30 cents before going over $30 and crashing back down to under $5.

By late 2013 the price had started climbing again and more speculators were being drawn into the market, seeing bitcoin as an opportunity to make some huge returns. The price topped out just under $1,200 that year, representing a 200X increase in the space of fewer than two years. However, by January 2015 the price fell back down to a low of $152, representing a decline of 87%!

These intense swings in price had the effect of drawing many people in as the price rose, only for everyone to once again declare Bitcoin dead after the price crashed. 2014 was a particularly bad year for the cryptocurrency, as the largest exchange at the time, Mt. Gox, shut down after announcing the theft of 850,000 bitcoin belonging to its users. At the time Mt. Gox handled around 70% of all bitcoin transactions worldwide so this was a significantly damaging event and as a result, the bitcoin price entered a long downward period.

Slowly, over time, confidence in bitcoin did start to reappear and many more exchanges came online in the following years, giving users much more choice around how they bought and sold their bitcoin. 2017 marked the peak to date in both bitcoin's price and familiarity among the general public as the price skyrocketed to its current all-time high of just under $20,000.

During the summer of 2017, there was a major software upgrade to the network, known as Segregated Witness or “SegWit”. This upgrade reduced the size of the blocks used in the protocol, to improve Bitcoin’s scalability and support the development of a second layer of code known as the Lightning Network. Changes to the Bitcoin protocol are implemented by a team of developers and any changes are subject to a stringent review process. Any changes must also be accepted by a majority of network participants, ensuring the network remains secure through its decentralized structure.

The upgrade put a lot of uncertainty in the market to rest, and within a matter of months demand soared and the price hit its peak. The 2017 peak was generally characterized by widespread euphoria as people thought the price would keep going up, almost vertically, forever. Bitcoin was being talked about in the mainstream media for the first time and started popping up in everyday conversations. Many people made their first cryptocurrency purchase in late 2017 dreaming of making their millions, and sure enough, within a few weeks the bubble burst and it all came crashing down.

Since then bitcoin has been in a period of downwards and sideways movement as the market resets for another potential run-up. While the price may have been fairly stagnant, there have been many significant developments in the space. Exchanges are becoming more reliable and user-friendly, and are suffering fewer attacks and losses of users’ funds. Futures contracts, a financial instrument that institutions typically utilize in their investments, are also now available for bitcoin, with some being listed on the Intercontinental Exchange, one of the largest in the world.

The cryptocurrency space is maturing and Bitcoin is being talked about more and more as a financial instrument; the world's first truly digital financial asset. It has certainly come a long way from the days of the cypherpunks and a handful of users on the fringes of the internet.

While the 2017 bubble was mainly driven by retail investors, primarily individuals looking to speculate, the groundwork is now being laid for institutional investors such as hedge funds to enter the market. These institutional players have *significantly* more capital available to invest than your average Joe. Bitcoin is now becoming accessible to them, and given its incredible returns over the past decade, and the fact that it is uncorrelated to other investment assets, it is becoming a very attractive option in the current uncertain economic climate.

The What Chapter Summary

- The Bitcoin whitepaper appeared online in 2008 and on 3rd January 2009, the genesis block was created.

- Bitcoin is a form of digital cash that can be transferred directly between two people over a decentralized network, without the need of a third party.

- All transactions ever made in bitcoin are recorded on a publicly available digital ledger known as a blockchain.

- Through the use of digital signatures, encryption, and decentralization, Bitcoin provides a solution to the double-spend problem by ensuring that each transaction can only be recorded once in the digital ledger.

- Little is known about the identity of Bitcoin's pseudonymous creator, Satoshi Nakamoto, but there are some known candidates who have been involved in Bitcoin from the beginning.

- Much like real-world cash, bitcoin is stored in a digital wallet, which can be either online or offline.

- Bitcoin is bought and sold through websites known as exchanges, where it can be transacted for other currencies such as dollars.

- A single bitcoin was originally worth fractions of a cent, before the price peaked just below $20,000 in 2017.

3. How

"Bitcoin is a technological tour de force."

- *Bill Gates, founder of Microsoft*

We now have a good idea of what Bitcoin is, how it was developed, and a small clue as to who created it. But to understand it fully, it is important to have some knowledge as to how the underlying technology works.

It is true that to use bitcoin, much like you would use the internet, you don't need to have any knowledge about how the technology actually works. As long as you can perform the actions you need to and it doesn't crash, then all is well. In fact, it is likely that the majority of bitcoin users don't fully understand how it works.

By all means, we don't need to go to extreme measures and learn how to code the thing, but a basic level of technical understanding is beneficial. Not least because these technological attributes are key to what makes Bitcoin unique, and what gives bitcoin their value.

Certainly from an investment perspective, it is a good idea to be knowledgeable about anything we invest in and the same applies to Bitcoin. If you know *how* it works, you can make a lot more sense of everything else you see or hear from others about it.

Blockchain

If you've read anything about Bitcoin and cryptocurrencies you've most likely heard of blockchain. This is the underlying technology behind cryptocurrencies which essentially makes them different from regular digital payments you can make through a bank.

The definition of blockchain is pretty straightforward. As we know, all transactions ever made in bitcoin are stored in a digital ledger that is maintained by the network. A block is a collection of data relating to activity in bitcoin, for example, a block would contain data regarding the time, date and amount of bitcoin moved, and which addresses it moved to and from. The chain is the collection of all the blocks, which then forms the digital ledger.

Think of blockchain like a book. A new block is like a new page that is being written. Once complete, that page is then bound into the spine of the book and given a sequential page number. Once it has been bound in place it can no longer be removed, edited, or moved.

So how does this work in practice? As transactions are made on the Bitcoin digital ledger they are recorded by all computers on the network. Those transactions are then combined in a block. For that block to be added to the blockchain, it requires a valid hash.

A hash is a 256-bit number that is generated from all the data within that block, combined with the hash from the previous block. Hashing is a form of cryptography, used to sign off a block of transactions. Once a block has been hashed it is not possible to change any data within that block without the hash changing and it is also not possible to ascertain what data went into that block from the hash itself.

However, if you have the valid transaction data, it is straightforward to verify that the hash has been generated from it. Therefore a majority of machines on the network can quickly verify that a block of transactions is valid based on the hash generated. Think of it like a maths equation, while it may take some time to solve initially, once you have solved it and can show your workings, it can be easily verified by others. Similarly, if you just have the solution, there is no way to figure out exactly what the workings were.

When a block is ready to be added to the blockchain the hash is validated in this way by a majority of the network. Once it has successfully been added to the blockchain, all the data within that block is publicly available to view as part of the digital ledger. Once your transaction has been hashed into a block it is said to have been confirmed. With every subsequent block that is added the transaction achieves an additional confirmation. Until your transaction has been picked up and hashed into a block in this way it is said to be unconfirmed. If it is never confirmed, eventually it will be rejected and the bitcoin returned to the address that sent them.

While it is possible to go back and change data in a previous block, that would then change its hash completely, and the hash of the next block and the next block and so on. It, therefore, requires a huge amount of computing power to go back and make changes to the digital ledger, making it virtually immutable.

Why is so much computing power required? Well, you can't add any old hash to a block. Each block contains a complicated maths puzzle as defined in Bitcoin's code, much harder than anything that could be solved by a human. Powerful computers known as miners search for solutions to these puzzles and when a valid hash solution is found, that hash can then be used to add the block to the blockchain.

With Bitcoin, a valid solution is usually found every 10 minutes or so, so every 10 minutes a new block is hashed and added to the blockchain. These blocks are limited in size to 1 megabyte, about the same as 1 minute of audio in MP3 format. Therefore each block can hold approximately 3,500 transactions. This system is known as a proof-of-work (PoW) system as blocks can only be added once the cryptographic puzzles are solved, requiring a high level of computing power, which translates into a high amount of electricity usage.

Blockchain technology underpins all cryptocurrencies but it is used in many different ways depending on the objectives of the developers of each. While other cryptocurrencies may claim to be better, faster, and more energy-efficient than Bitcoin, they simply do not share the same monetary properties. More on that later.

You may have heard blockchain talked about as the next big thing. Certainly, it seems to be a buzzword as the potential next life-changing technology to be discovered. In reality, for most uses blockchain is a slow and cumbersome solution that adds very little. While it provides a decentralized immutable ledger that safeguards against manipulation by a central authority, in many cases where blockchain is being touted as revolutionary it simply isn't necessary to have such a set-up. A normal database would suffice and would be a much quicker and efficient solution. Is there really a need for your utilities provider to store all their usage data in a decentralized database? No, of course not.

This distinction is very important. Many people discover Bitcoin and think it is blockchain that is the next big thing. It is, in fact, the opposite, the most compelling use case for blockchain is Bitcoin.

Nodes

The network is maintained on machines known as nodes. Anyone with a basic computer and an internet connection can run what is known as a "full node" by downloading the Bitcoin open-source software. After a lengthy initial download of the blockchain to date, your full node will then continue updating with new transactions as more blocks are added to the blockchain. Through your full node you can browse and explore the blockchain as you will have a record of every bitcoin transaction ever made.

The nodes obtain the information from other nodes on the network rather than a central source of information, and if your node goes offline it will just carry on where it left off the next time you connect to the internet, by downloading all the transactions that took place while it was offline. This is in essence what creates the truly decentralized nature of Bitcoin.

There are currently thousands of these nodes running and that number is likely to increase as bitcoin adoption continues to grow. Therefore, if a dishonest node tries to post false transactions to the ledger it can very quickly be identified as it's records will differ from those held by thousands of others on the network. This has the effect of making the Bitcoin network extremely secure as you have thousands of independent participants each monitoring the transactions that are being entered. Combined with the fact that it is very difficult to go back and alter blocks that have already been added to the blockchain, it is almost impossible to cheat the system.

Multiple decentralized nodes also make the network extremely reliable. So long as one node exists with a copy of the digital ledger, other nodes can re-join the network and start downloading the transactions again. Therefore to completely shut down the network every single node would need to be shut down. With thousands of nodes around the world in different countries with their own power sources and independent internet connections, it would take a truly cataclysmic event for them all to go down at once.

Even if this was to happen, unless they were all destroyed, once power and connectivity had been restored the network could restart where it left off. The Bitcoin blockchain is now also being transmitted via satellite, therefore even without internet access, you could run a full node through a satellite receiver.

Miners

In addition to nodes, the other main components in the Bitcoin network are miners. Miners are actually mining nodes. They function as nodes on the network but also have another important function; mining new bitcoin. The term "miner" can refer to either the computer that actually does the mining, or a person or group of people who run such machines to mine bitcoin.

As we know, each block in the blockchain contains a complicated maths puzzle based on 256-bit cryptography. These puzzles require a considerable amount of computing power to solve. Whenever a solution is found, the miner with the solution can hash the latest block onto the blockchain and as a result, receives a block reward made up of transaction fees for the transactions processed in that block and a quantity of new bitcoin.

This process of receiving the block reward effectively unlocks new bitcoin which did not previously exist. The transfer of these new bitcoin to the miner will be entered as the first transaction in the next block. This is why the practice is known as mining. It is a similar process to mining gold out of the ground with a pickaxe, with the miners doing all the hard work in cracking the cryptographic puzzle. Unlike mining gold, however, with bitcoin, you know how much your reward will be and you can reliably estimate how often you will receive one based on the mining power you have available.

It is believed that Satoshi intended that any ordinary

computer connected to the network would be able to mine for bitcoin. However, as the network developed and bitcoin became tradeable, more and more powerful computers were developed that were specifically designed to mine bitcoin.

While normal computers usually run off a central processing unit (CPU), it was quickly discovered that other types of computer could solve the cryptography puzzles much more efficiently and within a few years of Bitcoin launching, computers designed specifically for the purpose of mining were available to buy.

The most advanced machines these days use application-specific integrated circuits and are known as ASICs. It is estimated that today's ASICs are around 100 billion times quicker than the average CPU in 2009 when Bitcoin was launched!

Why have we seen such incredible advances in this technology? Simply put, because there is money to be made. If you can mine bitcoin more efficiently, you can get more bitcoin from the same amount of electricity. And more bitcoin means more profit. In essence, bitcoin is a currency based on energy. The only way to generate new bitcoin is through mining which is quite an energy-intensive task. Therefore, the drive for quicker miners is effectively just a push for energy efficiency.

If you want to make money mining bitcoin you effectively have two options; improve the efficiency of your mining equipment to mine more, or reduce the cost of your energy to ensure you can profit from your current level of mining. Miners who have access to cheap energy will do well, as will those who run the most advanced hardware. These days the mining landscape is so advanced that huge mining farms are being set-up with thousands and thousands of ASICs. Position one of these in a country with low energy costs and bitcoin mining can be big business.

Another development that Satoshi may not have anticipated is that of mining pools. While an individual who wants to mine cannot compete on cost with huge mining farms, if they all pool their resources together it can become considerably more worthwhile.

Mining pools combine the power of all participants' miners and any block rewards they receive are shared out among the participants in proportion to the amount of mining power each person contributes to the pool. The vast majority of bitcoin mining nowadays is done via mining pools.

Hash Rate

To unlock the block reward, miners must correctly solve the mathematical puzzle within each block. They solve this by repeatedly guessing solutions, known as hashes. The more solutions the miner can guess, the more likely that it will find the correct hash to solve the puzzle, allowing it to add the block to the blockchain and earn the block reward.

The speed at which it can guess solutions is known as the hash rate. This rate is usually a considerably large number and will normally be expressed as one of the following:

- MH/s - Mega hash, equivalent to 1 million hashes per second
- GH/s - Giga hash, equivalent to 1 billion hashes per second
- TH/s - Terra hash, equivalent to 1 trillion hashes per second
- PH/s - Peta hash, equivalent to 1,000 trillion hashes per second
- EH/s - Exa hash, equivalent to 1 million trillion, or a quintillion, hashes per second

The most advanced ASIC miners currently available run at around 110 TH/s and cost in the region of $3,000 to buy.

Based on the number and speed of blocks mined, it is

possible to estimate the total hash rate of all miners connected to the Bitcoin network. As of the time of writing, the total network hash rate was around 110 EH/s! Now that's a lot of computer power.

As the Bitcoin network continues to grow and more miners join, the hash rate will continue to grow. It can therefore be a useful metric to use to judge the overall strength of the network.

Difficulty

The concept of hash rate gives rise to a very valid question. We know that a new block is mined roughly every ten minutes, but surely if there are more computers mining, and those computers can mine faster and faster than ever, shouldn't the blocks be mined much quicker?

That is a completely accurate assumption. More hash power does mean blocks are mined more quickly. However, Satoshi obviously saw this coming because the Bitcoin code contains a very clever and very simple mechanism to ensure that blocks continue to be mined on average every ten minutes.

That mechanism is known as the difficulty adjustment. The mathematical puzzles that must be solved to mine a new block can be altered to vary the average number of hashes it will take to find a solution. After every 2,016 blocks mined the Bitcoin protocol makes an adjustment, based on a moving average that targets an average number of blocks per hour. 2,016 blocks at the average rate of ten minutes per block is equivalent to 14 days. So roughly every two weeks, the difficulty level is adjusted to try and keep the blocks coming at a nice steady rate of one every ten minutes.

The difficulty can go up or down, depending on whether more miners are joining or leaving the network. Let's look at an example. Let's say a huge mining farm came online all of a sudden that had the equivalent of 25% of the network's hashing power. All of a sudden, blocks would be being mined much quicker than normal due to the increased hash rate of the network. Rather than taking two weeks to mine 2,016 blocks, it might only take 11 days, if each block was mined in 8 minutes rather than 10. However, once those 2,016 blocks had been mined the difficulty would significantly increase and the rate at which new blocks were mined would drop back to one every 10 minutes.

If this massive mining farm then suddenly left the network, the hash rate would drop sharply and the time taken to mine new blocks would increase to well over 10 minutes. It would probably, therefore, take more than 14 days to mine the 2,016 blocks to reach the next difficulty adjustment. At that point, difficulty would then adjust down and the average time of 10 minutes per block would be restored once again.

This is a simple example and the chance of a major player with 25% of total hash rate dropping in and out of the network like this is extremely remote. However, the difficulty is continually adjusting based on the number of miners on the network and the overall hash rate.

The level of difficulty is denoted by a simple number. When Satoshi first ran Bitcoin the difficulty was 1. At the time of writing, the network has grown so large and powerful that difficulty has had to increase to over 16 trillion!

The Halving

You may well have heard of the Bitcoin halving, or halvening, as some people call it. This is another unique feature of Bitcoin which gives it its sound monetary properties.

We have talked about mining and we know that every time a new block is mined, the miner that successfully completes the puzzle receives the block reward. This is made up of some transaction fees and a number of new bitcoin. As the name suggests, this is in effect the miner's payment for maintaining the Bitcoin network. The network would not be around for long if it was reliant on the goodwill of miners to keep their energy-hungry mining machines running constantly at great expense.

This is an economic game. Miners are drawn in by the potential gains they can make by mining and selling the bitcoin they receive from the block rewards. Bitcoin mining is effectively a way that excess or cheap electricity can be converted into profit. Now, in the beginning, when bitcoin wasn't widely used and each bitcoin was worth peanuts, the block reward for each block was 50 bitcoin. That means for every block mined, one every ten minutes, 50 new bitcoin would be released to the miner that successfully solved the puzzle.

Given that in the early days it was virtually only Satoshi that was mining, you can probably start to see how he ended up with a wallet containing almost 1 million bitcoin!

Now, where does the halving come in? Satoshi recognized that to have any chance of becoming a global currency, bitcoin could not go on being mined in this quantity forever. A currency where the money supply keeps increasing simply doesn't make for sound money. More on that in the next chapter.

Satoshi decided that after every 210,000 blocks mined, or 4 years at an average of one block every 10 minutes, the number of bitcoin given out in the block reward would halve. So after the first halving, the reward halved from 50 per block to 25 per block, then after another 210,000 blocks, it reduced from 25 to 12.5, and so on. After the third halving on May 11th 2020, the block reward was reduced to 6.25 bitcoin for every block mined.

This pattern will continue until the maximum supply of 21 million bitcoin have been mined, sometime around the year 2140. This continual reduction also explains why over 18 million bitcoin have already been mined after 11 years of Bitcoin's existence, but it will take over 100 years for the remaining 3 million to be produced.

The impact of the halving on miners is that literally overnight their expected return of bitcoin from their mining operations is cut in half. Many miners become unprofitable at this point and leave the network, but this presents an opportunity for more efficient miners to join in their place. While this may seem hard on the miners, it should be noted that these halvings are hard-coded into Bitcoin, they will have had many years warning of this upcoming event.

The Mining Ecosystem

The miners, are in essence, the lifeblood of the Bitcoin network. Without miners, the network simply couldn't function. Bitcoin mining has formed its own ecosystem that pulls together all of the elements within the Bitcoin protocol to keep the network growing. Let's take a look at how it all fits together, and the impact mining has on the bitcoin price.

More miners tend to join the network when they see the price of bitcoin increasing. While miners' power is usually charged in dollars or other local currencies, they are effectively paid in the bitcoin they receive from block rewards. Therefore, as the bitcoin price increases, there is more money to be made as their costs remain the same but their revenue is increasing in dollar terms.

As most utility providers do not yet accept payment in bitcoin, it is typical that a miner will sell a portion of the bitcoin they mine to cover their electricity costs in dollars. Now, as more miners join the network the overall hash rate starts to increase. The difficulty adjusts upwards in an attempt to slow down block mining in the face of this increased hash rate.

What we have seen in the past is that once the bitcoin price gets going, it is very hard to stop. As the price increases, more and more speculators and investors are drawn into the market and it continues spiraling upwards. An increasing price attracts more miners and hash rate and difficulty both continue moving up sharply.

Eventually, the market peaks and the price bubble bursts. Investors start selling heavily and the price crashes. Now, the bitcoin price tends to move more quickly than the fortnightly difficulty adjustment, therefore, at this point many miners become unprofitable as the difficulty is still sky-high but the price is dropping rapidly. At this time many miners will decide to turn off their machines and what is sometimes known as "miner capitulation" ensues. The reduced number of miners results in a sharp drop in hash rate and those miners that are left may choose to sell even more bitcoin than usual to capitalize before the price drops further.

The sudden drop in hash rate will trigger a downwards difficulty adjustment, making it easier to mine each block. Eventually, the market will level out as more miners rejoin to capitalize on the lower difficulty level. The market reaches some form of equilibrium and the bitcoin price will go through a period of relative stability.

So what triggers these run-ups in the bitcoin price? That's where the halving comes in. The immediate impact of the halving is that many miners are no longer profitable as their revenue is cut in half. These miners will shut off and the network hash rate and difficulty will drop as a result. Reduced difficulty presents an opportunity for more efficient, more powerful miners to come online and mine profitably. It is also favorable to miners who have access to cheap electricity. Over time, the mining infrastructure will become more efficient which is positive for the network as a whole.

The main impact of the halving is that the number of

new bitcoin created is reduced by 50%. Therefore, while the overall supply of bitcoin is still increasing, it is increasing considerably more slowly than before. A simple understanding of economics will tell you that slowing supply growth while demand continues to increase, generally leads to the price only going up.

The price tends to grind upwards slowly at first, before it starts to garner more and more attention, leading investors to buy-in and the cycle repeats. With each of these cycles to date, the extreme volatility in the bitcoin price has reduced slightly from the cycle before as the cryptocurrency ecosystem continues to mature. After each major correction, the price has eventually found a floor not far from its "production cost", the average cost at which a miner can mine a new bitcoin. With each halving this production cost increases as fewer bitcoin are being released from each block.

Over time, as the overall value of bitcoin increases, these bubbles and subsequent crashes should become less severe and in the long-term, you might expect the bitcoin price to eventually plateau.

Proof Of Work (POW) Vs Proof Of Stake (POS)

The hashing algorithm Bitcoin uses is known as proof of work (POW). While Bitcoin wasn't created until 2009, the concept of proof of work has been around considerably longer. POW works in a very simple way. The puzzles that miners must solve to add the next block to the blockchain are solved through brute force. This means the more guesses you have at a solution, the more likely you are to find the correct hash. No miner can gain an advantage over another through any means other than having more computational power.

This means POW systems tend to be very energy and capital intensive. While the puzzles are hard to solve, the solutions can be very easily verified by the network, as a simple hash is produced as the output.

POW also helps keep the network secure, as in order to post a malicious entry to the digital ledger any dishonest miner would need a majority of the hashing power of the network. They would need 51% of all computational power on the network. This is an enormous amount of processing power and it makes an attack on the network economically unviable, as doing so would be prohibitively expensive and any such attack would immediately devalue bitcoin due to the breach of network security.

Proof of stake (POS) systems are a newer development and some newer cryptocurrencies other than Bitcoin make use of them. POS systems also verify and add blocks to the blockchain just like Bitcoin, however, the way in which the blocks are validated differs. Rather than miners trying to solve complicated puzzles, a miner is selected in some determined way based on the number of coins that they hold. For example, a user with 50 coins would be 5 times more likely to be selected than a user with 10 coins.

Another key difference of POS is that no new coins are necessarily mined with each new block. Whether any new coins are produced at all, depends on the individual cryptocurrency. Sometimes users can earn rewards by staking their coins, holding them in a particular wallet to enable them to be used to support the security and operations of the blockchain. This works much like holding money in a bank account to receive interest.

Both systems have their advantages and disadvantages. A big criticism of POW systems like Bitcoin is that mining is heavily energy-intensive and huge amounts of electricity are consumed, whereas POS systems are much more energy-efficient.

Another criticism of POW systems is that they tend to move more towards centralization than POS. Generally speaking, the more a miner invests mining bitcoin, the greater share of the network power they will control. The biggest players can gain economies of scale, which for every $1000 invested would yield them a greater return than the average person running a miner at home. Whereas with POS the share of network power is distributed evenly based only on the amount invested. An additional $1000 invested would yield the same network control regardless of who invested it.

However, POS has one significant drawback, known as the "Nothing at Stake" problem. Occasionally blockchains fork (more on this in a moment), which means that the blockchain splits into two separate blockchains. One being the "original" and the other being a separate fork that starts adding its own blocks of transactions onto the existing blockchain. With a fork, comes the creation of a new cryptocurrency and users receive the same value in the new cryptocurrency as they previously held in the original.

With a POW system, miners have the choice to mine the original cryptocurrency or switch to the new fork, but they can't mine both. They are said to have something at stake. This discourages forks which is generally considered to be a good thing as one powerful network is more useful than many less powerful ones. However, with a POS system, a user can stake their cryptocurrency on both networks following a fork. They effectively have nothing at stake, as they are not required to spend time and energy mining.

Forks

Blockchain forks happen when a change in the current code is required. Why would such a change be needed? It could be for many reasons, but generally, it will be for some purpose of improving the blockchain's functionality.

A fork is equivalent to a new blockchain branching out from the existing one. All the historical transactions will still be there but one blockchain will continue with the original code and the fork will continue with the new code.

Think of it as a game. Everyone must agree to the rules to play but when a dispute arises about what those rules should be, you may find that the players split and start playing two different games with different rules. Forks can be hard or soft. Soft forks still work well with the old rules and were used to resolve issues such as the Value Overflow incident previously discussed. Soft forks are effectively the equivalent of a software upgrade that is rolled out across the network.

Hard forks are an entirely different ball game. These are major changes to the rules and effectively create a new blockchain altogether. A new blockchain means a new cryptocurrency will be created. Holders of the original cryptocurrency will receive the equivalent number of coins in this new cryptocurrency as a result of the fork. For example, if Bitcoin were to fork, you would receive one new coin for every bitcoin you held. On a POW system, miners have the choice to continue mining the original or switch to the new one. Ultimately, the choice of the miners will determine which network goes on to become the strongest.

Bitcoin has been through a number of forks in its time, including several hard forks. You may have heard of Bitcoin Cash, Bitcoin SV (Satoshi Vision), or Bitcoin Gold. These are all hard forks from the original Bitcoin blockchain. Bitcoin SV was actually a subsequent hard fork from Bitcoin Cash which was already a hard fork from the original Bitcoin.

These forks generally arise when there is a disagreement among the developers over which way the technology should be advanced. The Bitcoin Cash hard fork arose over a disagreement over block size. Bitcoin Cash proponents felt a larger block size would be beneficial as more transactions could be processed in each block, making it more useful as a medium of exchange. The drawback of larger blocks is that more computational power is required to run a full node, making it inaccessible for many.

The Almighty 51%

Given that Bitcoin has no central authority and no one person in charge you may be wondering how all these software changes and forks get implemented. In the early days, most updates would be actioned by Satoshi himself, who would then ask all network participants to download the updated protocol. As there weren't many users at the time this worked well. However, when Satoshi left the project this responsibility to maintain the code was passed over to a team of Bitcoin Core developers.

While the Bitcoin code is open source and many developers contribute ideas and submit code, it is only these Bitcoin Core developers who have access to actually commit changes to the code. Over time, a more formal process has been created to organize, review, and debate potential improvements. Nowadays, any change is submitted as a Bitcoin Improvement Proposal (BIP) and reviewed by the Bitcoin community. Only when a BIP has been thoroughly vetted and any objections resolved, is it passed for implementation on the blockchain.

Now, you still might think that these Bitcoin Core developers have a huge amount of power to be able to amend the code themselves, and that is true, however, being a decentralized network, any implemented changes must have a consensus of approval to be enacted. For soft forks to be adopted a majority of mining power on the network must be running a client that recognizes the fork. Therefore, if less than 50% of mining power adopts, the soft fork will not be implemented. Any malicious or unsolicited changes by the developers would simply be ignored by the network.

Where this consensus cannot be reached and there remains a group of miners that want radical changes to the code, it will more than likely result in a hard fork, and the formation of a completely new blockchain.

While powerful users cannot simply implement their own changes to the Bitcoin source code or force others to adopt a particular client, if a miner were to hold over 50% of the network's mining power, they could choose to block or reverse transactions on the blockchain and potentially double-spend coins as a result. This is known as a 51% attack.

Such an attack could enable the powerful miner to mess with current transactions and double-spend coins but it would still not enable them to go back and amend previously mined blocks. Therefore, this type of attack would not completely destroy Bitcoin but it would cause a huge crisis of confidence in the technology, which would be severely damaging.

While possible, the chances of any such attack are considered remote. A would-be attacker would need to invest a huge sum of money to obtain 50% of the mining power. Attacking the network in this way, would likely significantly reduce the value of bitcoin, diminishing not only the value of any coins they had double-spent but also all of the investment they had made in mining infrastructure.

Any miner with 50% of the network power would almost certainly be better off financially just continuing to mine new bitcoin. In fact, back in 2014, one mining pool did briefly exceed 50% of Bitcoin mining power. Recognizing the threat this might pose, they voluntarily chose to reduce their capacity and agreed not to go above 40% of the network's hash power in future.

Wallets

Once you own some bitcoin, you'll need somewhere to store it. Just like normal cash, bitcoin is stored in a wallet, a digital wallet. Bitcoin never actually leave the network. The digital ledger simply keeps track of how many bitcoin are at each address within it. Every node maintains a copy of the entire ledger so everyone is in agreement about the location of all bitcoin.

A wallet, therefore, is simply a collection of addresses on the network that belong to you. You can use your wallet to generate new addresses which can then be shared with people who want to send you bitcoin.

In addition to addresses, the wallet also contains your public and private keys. The public keys are used to generate addresses, effectively working like a bank account number. Therefore, it doesn't matter if your public keys are shared with others. However, in order to spend any bitcoin from your wallet, you need to sign off the transaction with your private keys. Therefore, it is essential that you keep the private keys safe and do not share them with anyone.

If your private keys are shared or lost you could find your bitcoin being stolen or "lost" forever. In this instance, when we say lost, your bitcoin would effectively be locked in your wallet forevermore, unable to be moved. To continue the bank account analogy, think of the private key as a PIN.

Keys take the form of a 256-bit alphanumeric string, a

collection of 64 letters and numbers, however, they can be converted into more user-friendly forms such as QR codes.

The most basic form of wallet is paper-based, simply print or write down your keys and you're set. Because bitcoin never actually leave the network, you don't necessarily need a computer to store them. Once they are in your wallet address, so long as you have a paper copy of the keys, they are secure. You will, of course, need a device connected to the network to spend them when the time comes. Despite their simplicity, paper wallets are actually very secure as they are completely offline and therefore unhackable. The risk is that the keys get lost, destroyed, or found by someone that shouldn't have them.

You can also buy hardware wallets which are small devices that connect to the network when you need to make transactions. These are also quite secure because they are offline most of the time, but remain susceptible to loss, damage, or theft.

Alternatively, you can get software wallets that run on a computer or smartphone. These are convenient but have the added security risk that the device could be hacked, in addition to being lost or stolen.

Finally, you can use an online wallet. These score best for convenience as, with the right password, you can access your bitcoin from any device with an internet connection, but you are then completely trusting of a third party as the keys themselves will be held on their servers. Even if the wallet provider is well-intentioned, such a service will attract a lot of attention from hackers, therefore, they must also have very robust cybersecurity measures in place.

That might all sound a little scary to you, but there are steps you can take to minimize the risk of loss. You can keep backups of your wallets and keys just in case the worst should happen. Many wallets can also be backed up using a seed phrase which will be a collection of 12 or 24 words. Should your computer crash or be thrown out of the window, you can install a wallet on a new machine and back it up from the phrase. Being only 12 or 24 words this could even be memorized. As with your private keys, if written down your seed phrase should be kept private and not shared with anyone!

It is true that individual custody is one of Bitcoin's biggest strengths, however, many people would prefer the security of third party custody, as with banks today. As cryptocurrency adoption grows, it is almost certain that reliable third party custody solutions will start to be developed as part of the infrastructure.

Exchanges

Once you have a wallet set up, you're ready to buy some bitcoin. Bitcoin is obtained mainly in two ways, it can either be mined or purchased from an exchange. Exchanges are simply websites that bring together buyers and sellers of cryptocurrencies in the same way stock market exchanges enable people to trade stocks.

Cryptocurrency exchanges are set up with a number of different wallets that store users' funds. You log in as with any website with an email address and a password and then have access to move funds in and out of your account. Although the funds are in your account, be aware that in terms of their on-chain location, they are sitting in the exchange's wallet. This is vital to understand. If you do not have your funds in your own wallet and do not have ownership of the private keys, effectively you don't own those coins.

If the exchange goes offline you have no way of accessing your funds. It is therefore highly recommended that you do not leave any cryptocurrency on an exchange account. You should transfer your funds off into a secure wallet if you do not intend to transact with those funds for any period of time.

Exchanges almost work like a bank in that respect. You have a login which effectively acts as an IOU to the funds in your account, but they remain in possession of the exchange. While this may seem more convenient than transferring into a wallet, you run the risk of the exchange going down, or worse, being hacked, and your coins lost. While exchange security is improving all the time, there is a long list of exchange hacks that should serve as a stark warning.

Some people leave their bitcoin on an exchange because they actively trade it against other cryptocurrencies. In these cases, the convenience can outweigh the risk but it is ultimately up to the individual to assess the risk and act accordingly.

The Lightning Network

One subject that has caused more debate than any other in the Bitcoin developer community is around scalability and block size. There is no escaping the fact that with one block mined every ten minutes, you are waiting some time for your transaction to be confirmed. And that is just for one confirmation, if you are waiting for 2, 3 or 4 confirmations you could be waiting for up to an hour or so. In fact, the Bitcoin blockchain is limited to a paltry 7 transactions per second. By comparison, Visa can handle a peak in the region of 50,000 transactions per second!

This is a problem when it comes to using bitcoin as a medium of exchange for payments. It would be hard to argue that bitcoin is the future of money if you had to stand at the checkout at the grocery store for 20 minutes, while you waited for your payment to confirm. This problem is widely recognized and can be avoided by using a blockchain with bigger block sizes or more regular mining of blocks. Certainly, many other cryptocurrencies have been developed that are much quicker than Bitcoin at processing and confirming transactions.

This is where the Lightning Network comes in. As the name suggests, this is an additional layer on the Bitcoin blockchain that is designed to be fast. Ideal for processing transactions of any size quickly and cheaply.

The key distinction here is that the Lightning Network is *off-chain*. Unlike regular bitcoin transactions that are all recorded *on the chain*, Lightning transactions are recorded in a separate network of bi-directional payment channels that sits atop the Bitcoin blockchain.

Now, what on earth is a bi-directional payment channel? In effect, it's just a ledger between two people or entities. Transactions on the Lightning Network get recorded in this ledger and only when the balances that each hold, are confirmed by both people, are they recorded onto the blockchain. To use the Lightning Network you simply send some bitcoin to your own Lightning wallet which can then be transferred to other Lightning wallets on the network.

It remains trustless as the payments are routed through its own nodes and governed by the shared ledger, known technically as a smart contract. As more channels are formed, the network will route payments in the most efficient way possible, making it lightning fast. While it remains secure, it is not quite as secure as confirming an on-chain transaction in full on the blockchain. Its primary use is therefore considered to be small everyday payments, whereas, it would be considered wise to process larger payments on-chain and seek multiple confirmations.

The main benefit of transacting off-chain is, of course, the speed and scalability of the network. Transactions can be processed in milliseconds to seconds and it is believed that it can scale to the region of over 1 million transactions per second.

The Lightning Network is a relatively new development but is growing fast. As of April 2020, there were over 12,000 online nodes, 30,000+ active channels and it had a payment capacity of 920 bitcoin.

The How Chapter Summary

- All transactions made in bitcoin are stored on a digital ledger known as a blockchain, new blocks of transactions are added every ten minutes to the end of the "chain".

- The network is hosted worldwide on machines known as nodes. Anyone can run a node and there are now thousands active around the world.

- Miners solve complex math puzzles to add a block to the chain, the successful miner is rewarded with newly mined bitcoin.

- The speed at which miners can guess solutions to the puzzle is known as the hash rate, and the aggregate hash rate of the entire Bitcoin network can be reliably estimated.

- After every 2,016 blocks mined (around every 2 weeks) the difficulty of the math puzzles adjusts to make them easier or harder depending on the current hash rate of the network.

- A Halving occurs after every 210,000 blocks mined (around 4 years) when the number of bitcoin miners receive for solving the puzzles is cut in half.

- Bitcoin utilizes a proof-of-work system as miners must show that they have successfully solved the puzzle to mine each block.

- Sometimes cryptocurrencies fork and the blockchain splits into two; other versions of Bitcoin have been created in this way.

- Changes to the protocol can be enacted by certain developers but they are reliant on a majority of network participants accepting the change for it to take effect.

- Bitcoin is held in wallets that can be online or offline, holding the public and private keys that enable bitcoin to be transferred across the network.

- Exchanges enable people to buy and sell cryptocurrencies using other currencies such as dollars.

- The Lightning Network is currently being developed as an off-chain solution for quick and cheap transactions.

4. Why

"With the exception only of the period of the gold standard, practically all governments of history have used their exclusive power to issue money to defraud and plunder the people."

- *Friedrich A. Hayek, economist, and advocate of Austrian economics*

We have discovered what Bitcoin is and how it works. But why might we need it? Why is it any different from other forms of currency? Why is a single bitcoin worth thousands of dollars?

Digital payments can already be made at the touch of a button through banking apps on a laptop or even the most basic smartphone. There already exist hundreds of national currencies that serve the purposes of our day-to-day spending and investing.

In fact, some nations such as China, are already developing and testing a cryptocurrency form of their own national currency, a digital Yuan. So, with all these currencies available, why would we need bitcoin, or any of the thousands of other cryptocurrencies that have been created in the last decade?

Bitcoin is different. Fundamentally different.

Not just because it is a cryptocurrency. There are huge numbers of other cryptocurrencies that also use blockchain technology. The technology, although revolutionary for its time, has been copied and improved upon since.

The key difference, and where bitcoin derives its real value, is in its economic properties. To understand these properties, we need to explore the origins of money and the many different forms money has taken up until the present day.

Scarcity

Economics as a "science" is a relatively new field in the overall timespan of human development. It is a man-made creation. The "economy" is a collection of numbers and figures that economists have found ways to measure and compile into data sets.

Certainly, throughout the 20th and 21st centuries, the practice has become more and more complex, with endless tools and indicators being created to measure this economy. Nations take great pride in having a strong economy, therefore, it is perhaps not surprising that governments place great importance on maintaining the economy, at all costs.

But let's take a step back. What really drives the economy?

The fundamental principle of economics is one of scarcity. Indeed, the basic economic problem is how do you balance scarce resources with theoretically limitless wants? Limitless wants, are just that. Without constraints, humans are naturally inclined to want more and more. This is a natural survival instinct.

Our cave-dwelling ancestors would not know where the next meal was coming from, so, as the saying goes, you've got to "make hay while the sun shines". That means, when food is available you should consume as much as possible because you don't know how long you might be waiting for your next meal. This instinct is still in effect today and many Western countries now struggle with obesity epidemics partly because the "sun shines" all the time; food is readily available and over-consumed.

The greatest and ultimate constraint is time. Time can only be spent once, no matter who you are. If the hunter-gatherer spends all their time hunting for food and neglects to sleep or build shelter, they may have a lot of food, but they still won't survive for very long.

Our ancestors had to effectively use their time (a scarce resource) to meet their basic needs (wants) of survival and reproduction. Despite all the complexities of the modern world, this basic principle still holds true. Except now we exchange our time for money by working and use that money to meet our wants.

Similar examples of this can be seen in the animal kingdom. Without consciously knowing it, lions on the plains of Africa must balance their time between hunting, resting, and seeking out a mate to procreate with.

Humans differ in that we have developed the ability for foresight. We have learned that if we spend time creating a sharpened spear, or a fishing net, we will be able to catch much more food in the same amount of time, while potentially also expending less energy.

The hunter who spends a day foraging for twine, and then another day weaving that twine into a net, may go hungry for a couple of days, but will subsequently eat well for weeks, now that he has a means of catching more fish.

You could argue that this is a very early rudimentary form of capitalism. The hunter has spent resources (time and twine) and converted them into a capital item, an asset (the fishing net). This asset can then be used in the future for his own gain, to catch more fish.

Those cave-dwellers who were able to grasp this concept and make the best use of the scarce resources available to them, greatly increased their chances of survival and reproduction as they would be stronger, more healthy, and better able to provide for a family. It is, therefore, this effective use of scarce resources that has driven the human race forward.

Fast-forward back to the present day and this is still clear to see. Businesses and industries that can make better use of scarce resources tend to do very well. Motor cars are much quicker than horse and cart, saving time, and now they are everywhere. Electric cars are now also booming in popularity as they can be powered from a renewable power source, reducing the consumption of a scarce resource, oil.

The internet and modern technology have created all manner of different ways in which we can communicate, which saves us the time and energy of meeting face-to-face. In fact, many of these new technologies make previously impossible things possible, such as video calling someone on the other side of the planet. This is a good example of our insatiable wants being met.

Going back to our early ancestral example, let's now look at how the earliest forms of trade would have taken place. Let's say our fisherman has become so proficient at catching fish that he has an abundance, more than he needs to feed himself and his family. However, he may not know the first thing about climbing trees to collect apples.

Meanwhile, a neighboring neanderthal might be an expert at scaling the high branches to collect the juiciest ripe apples. He finds himself in a similar predicament, he can pick more than enough apples to feed himself and his family, but he couldn't catch a fish to save his life.

To get the nutrients they need and want, both families would benefit from a trade. Fish for apples. Apples for fish. The only thing left to agree on is the price. Let's say, on an average day, each could collect 5 fish or 50 apples respectively. After some bartering, they may then agree on an exchange of 1 fish for 10 apples. A deal has been struck.

Both parties are happy because they have exchanged what is an abundant resource for them, for something less abundant. They have both effectively used resources available to them to procure something that would otherwise have been unobtainable; they have met a new want.

This method of trade works well with certain goods. In the example above, both goods are perishable and of a similar value, and can be exchanged at a single point in time. Now, let's say a third cave-dweller has developed a method of hunting and skinning animals. He can use the fur-lined skin to make blankets, or clothing, that is much warmer than any other material readily available.

Catching and skinning an animal is a difficult and labor intensive task and the skin then needs to be fastened into shape to make clothing. He may be the only person able to do this for hundreds of miles, therefore, his fur clothing is very scarce and very valuable as it greatly increases the chances of surviving a cold winter.

It is so valuable in fact, that one piece of fur clothing could take the same amount of effort to produce, as collecting 1,000 apples, or catching 100 fish. This causes a problem. It now becomes very difficult to trade through barter. No-one would be willing to sell a fur blanket for 1,000 apples, or 100 fish, because these items will perish long before they can be consumed by a small family.

They could potentially strike a deal whereby 1 fish is provided each day for 100 days in exchange for a blanket, but then at what point would the blanket be handed over? Either the fisherman must trust that the blanket maker will keep good on his promise to deliver after 100 days, or the blanket maker must deliver upfront and hope that the fisherman continues to provide fish for 100 days.

They could meet in the middle and hand over the blanket after 50 days, however, this still requires an element of trust on both sides of the transaction, and could still leave either one out of pocket.

To provide a more modern-day example, let's say you are a shoemaker and you wish to buy a house to live in. No-one in their right mind would sell a house in exchange for shoes. Such a deal would leave the seller with thousands of pairs of shoes which they would then have to try and exchange for goods they actually want.

This is a fundamental problem of the barter method of transacting. Both parties must hold an item that the other wants, in economic speak, this is known as the "double coincidence of wants". And in the real world, it is surprisingly uncommon.

In order to progress economically and as a society, we, therefore, needed a medium of exchange. Something that would be universally recognized to have value, that could be easily exchanged in different quantities for any type of goods or service.

Money was born.

What Is Money?

This is something that we don't often ask. We all use money in our day to day life and think nothing of it. We don't stop and think about what it actually is, what properties it should have, or why it holds value.

In a literal sense, money as we know it, is small pieces of paper. Or numbers on a computer screen as you check your online balance. It is something of a self-fulfilling prophecy, it has value because we all accept that it has value. By using money in exchange for real goods or services, we can see this value in the real world.

To be an effective currency, it is generally accepted that money should have three key characteristics:

Medium of Exchange

Quite simply, this means the currency should be accepted in return for goods and services, "real" items. All parties to a transaction agree that the money in question can be used for this purpose.

Unit of Account

Money should have a standard unit by which it is measured. Ideally, this should also be divisible, countable, and fungible. For example, a dollar can be divided into 100 cents and is also easily countable. It is fungible because it can easily be replaced with another identical dollar.

A bad example of a unit of account would be grains of rice. Each one will be slightly different in size and shape and they are not divisible.

Store of Value

Money should retain a stable worth in terms of what it can be used to purchase; its purchasing power. Currency isn't much use if, after a few years in a savings account, it has not held any value.

Stores of value are not restricted just to currency. Precious metals such as gold tend to hold value over time well, as can many other items such as real estate, antiques, or classic cars.

Currencies are usually much less volatile than other asset classes which makes them a very safe store of value. That said, there have been numerous examples in history of hyperinflation, where a currency rapidly declines in purchasing power. We will look at this in more detail later.

The items most commonly used to function as forms of money have historically been coins and banknotes:

Coins

It is believed that money in its earliest form was used by the Chinese around 770 B.C. Rather than exchanging actual weapons and tools, they started using small bronze replicas. However, given their sharp and pointy design, over time, these were abandoned for a smoother shape, a coin.

It wasn't long before the first coins were officially minted in nearby Lydia, modern-day Turkey, by King Alyattes in 600 B.C. These first coins were made from a naturally occurring mixture of gold and silver, and enabled Lydia to increase trade and become one of the richest empires of its time.

For the next 1,000 years, coins would be the dominant form of money. As we know, they became so commonplace that they are still in use in most countries today.

One of the most attractive qualities of coins is that they can be minted from precious metals, which act as a very good store of value because they are not easily obtainable. Indeed the first coins were quite literally "worth their weight in gold" because they would have been minted from the precious metal itself, a practice which has long since been abandoned.

Notes

The Chinese were also the first to develop paper notes for use as currency, during the Tang dynasty between 618 A.D. and 907 A.D. This predates their use in Europe and elsewhere, where they didn't become widely used until the 17th century.

The Chinese recognized that it wasn't efficient to carry around heavy coins, particularly for merchants who may have accumulated a lot of wealth. Under the paper note system, merchants could deposit their coins with a trusted agent who would record the amount deposited on paper, a form of IOU. This could then be shown when buying goods so that the selling merchant knew they were able to pay at a later date.

It wasn't long before the Chinese government started accepting deposits in exchange for paper notes, and the first official paper currency was born. Paper currencies were in effect an IOU system. The paper notes themselves had no intrinsic value, but they did carry a promise from the government to convert the paper notes into the underlying precious metals.

Money Problems

Whilst money solved the problems of trade by barter, government-issued money brought with it new challenges.

Early coins were made purely from the precious metal from which they derived their value, typically gold or silver. However, rulers soon realized that they could melt down the existing coins, mix them with other more readily available metals such as copper or lead, and re-issue the coins at the same face value.

They could, therefore, produce more coins using the same overall amount of gold or silver. With each coin having the same face value, the sovereign now has more money at its disposal. They have effectively increased the money supply, the total *face value* of all coins in circulation.

This is a practice known as debasement. One of the most well-known examples of this was in the ancient Roman empire. The Denarius was the standard silver Roman coin of the time. When introduced around 211 B.C. it was virtually pure silver, however, over the next 500 years, it would undergo numerous debasements until the silver content was only 5%.

Why did Roman emperors do this? To fund their own interests. Palaces and wars need to be paid for somehow. As the Roman empire grew it became increasingly difficult to plunder silver and gold from neighboring countries, which meant spending was limited. It was much easier to raise money by debasing coins than by raising taxes, for example.

What was the impact of this debasement? The impact of any debasement is an increase in the money supply, as mentioned. While the *real value* of goods and services in an economy remains the same, there are now more coins to go around. The availability and supply of real goods and services haven't changed, however, demand has been artificially increased through the creation and spending of this new money.

As this new money trickles down through the economy, the increased number of coins means that the same goods and services start to cost more. The purchasing power of a single coin has been diminished. We have inflation.

Inflation is a sustained increase in the general price level of goods and services in an economy, over a period of time. Nowadays, in developed economies, inflation occurs slowly, maybe 1-2% per year. This means those goods and services you buy today will cost an additional 1-2% a year from now.

Relatively low inflation like this does not have a dramatic impact on consumers, but it does diminish purchasing power over time. If your wages are not increasing in line with inflation, and you have your life savings in an account with an interest rate lower than the rate of inflation, your money is actually losing value. Your wealth can purchase fewer real goods or services.

Governments and central banks target a small amount of inflation. Why? Because the mindset that your money is losing value in a savings account incentivizes spending. Governments love spending because it contributes to Gross Domestic Product (GDP). This is the aggregate spending of the entire economy and is the most commonly used yardstick to judge an economy's health. Rightly or wrongly, it is widely considered that a country with strong GDP growth each year is more prosperous.

So what became of our debasing Roman emperors? They failed to recognize the damaging impact their behavior was having on the economy of the empire. With dwindling supplies of gold and silver, they continued to debase the currency to fund the empire, resulting in catastrophic price rises in goods and services. By the 3rd century A.D., the economy was paralyzed and the empire had started its demise. The Romans had suffered the first known episode of hyperinflation.

While low inflation may be bearable, history is littered with episodes where inflation has become rampant and developed into hyperinflation. Hyperinflation is technically defined as when the prices of goods and services rise more than 50% *per month*. 50%?! Yes, that's right, your $4 coffee today would cost $6 next month, $9 the month after that, and so on.

Hyperinflation spirals out of control and is crippling to economies. The economy simply can't function when its currency is rapidly losing value. Panic buying ensues as people try to start hoarding goods in fear that they will cost more tomorrow. Cash in savings becomes worthless.

Banks and lenders run out of cash as people stop depositing in favor of spending. Unemployment rises as firms go bankrupt and the government subsequently has less tax revenue, forcing the government to create even more money to pay its bills. The vicious cycle continues. It can only be described as an economic and social disaster.

The Chinese suffered a similar fate with their first banknotes. Although they were well advanced, being some 500 years ahead of the rest of the world in using notes rather than coins, they made the fatal mistake of printing too many paper notes, leading to crippling hyperinflation. By the mid-15th century, they had abandoned paper money altogether, and would not return to it for several hundred years.

The early days of money demonstrated some issues. Namely, that the reigning powers found it difficult to resist the lure of debasement or money printing. You may, therefore, think that money was doomed to repeat this hyperinflationary cycle time and time again. However, in the ensuing period up until 1920, there was only one other example of hyperinflation, in France in 1795.

This hyperinflation in France was caused by counterfeit currency, rather than an intentional increase in the money supply by the government.

To give some further perspective, in the period from 1920 to the present day, there have been 57 documented cases of hyperinflation around the world.

So what changed in 1920 and how was hyperinflation prevented so effectively before that?

The Gold Standard

Following the minting of the first coins by the Lydians in 600 B.C., it wasn't long before they figured out how to create pure gold coins by separating the gold and silver from the original coins. These new coins derived their value from the actual weight of the gold used to forge them.

Gold was a rare metal, which meant it made a good store of value, and thus a good currency. Mining gold was a difficult and labor intensive task, and that was if you even knew where to dig! The average person could not easily obtain it and as a result, it held its value very effectively.

The key property of gold which ensures it retains value, is that it has a very high stock-to-flow ratio. We will look at this in more detail shortly.

It is worth noting that gold was selected not so much by design but rather by default. It was found to work as effective money through practice rather than through any sort of study of economics. It is quite clear that the Romans did not fully understand the properties that made gold sound money.

Adopting a "gold standard" basically means a country would equate its money, in whatever form that may take, to the amount of gold that it holds. At first, the gold was physically used as money and denoted by its weight, but towards the end of the 19th century, more and more nations started issuing paper currency that could be redeemed for a fixed amount of gold.

The gold standard incentivized nations to explore, as the more gold they could stockpile, the wealthier they would become. It was a key driver of the European exploration of the New World and it prompted several gold rushes in the US during the 1800s.

As nations began to formalize their own national currencies, the gold standard enabled these different paper currencies to be tied to a common underlying asset. By the end of the 19th century, the majority of developed nations had adopted the gold standard and it was working very effectively.

The gold standard solved the problem of inflation as countries could not print paper money if they did not have the corresponding amount of gold in their reserves. Therefore, to fund spending, governments had to raise money another way, primarily through taxes. This held governments accountable because if they were trying to raise taxes for a purpose that the public did not support, they would soon find themselves out of office.

Indeed, the gold standard oversaw a time of great political and economic stability. It was more difficult for leaders to raise taxes to fight unnecessary wars, rather nations focused on greater productivity at home. It was a period of great achievement as the industrial revolution brought about many technological developments and advances.

Unfortunately, all that was to change in 1914 with the outbreak of World War I. In order to fund the war effort, the gold standard was suspended by many countries so that money could be readily printed to finance military activity. This was a significant contributing factor that elongated the war as governments were able to continue funding battle, even if the public were not prepared to pay for it through increased taxes.

Following the end of the war, Germany experienced rampant hyperinflation as they struggled to pay down the excessive repatriations handed down to them by the Allies. The hyperinflation of the early 1920s in the Weimar Republic is one of the best-known cases of hyperinflation and much has been written about this topic.

Many countries tried to go back onto the gold standard following the war, but this was a difficult task as it would mean devaluing their currencies significantly. The number of notes in circulation had risen drastically but the amount of gold held in their reserves was relatively unchanged, meaning that the public would be forced to accept a reduction in the value of the currency they held.

Some countries did manage to go back on to the gold standard but the Great Depression in the US in the 1930s, resulted in the US coming off again. A decision which arguably exacerbated the situation rather than improving it.

The period between World War I and World War II was punctuated with examples of hyperinflation throughout Europe. It wasn't until after the Second World War that a gold standard, of sorts, was firmly re-established.

That new standard was known as the Bretton Woods system, named after the conference at which the world's greatest powers came to the agreement in 1944. The system was agreed upon between the United States, Canada, Western European countries, Japan, and Australia. The main motivation for the new system was to address the economic problems that had blighted the interwar period from 1918 to 1939 and ultimately led to the Second World War.

Bretton Woods can be summarized quite simply. All currencies would be pegged at a certain exchange rate to the US dollar, which would become the world's reserve currency. The US dollar itself, would be redeemable for gold. Therefore, all countries were effectively operating a gold standard as their currencies could be exchanged for US dollars at a set rate, which could then be converted to gold at a set rate.

As the gold standard had before, the Bretton Woods system worked very effectively and presided over a long period of economic stability. In fact, after the turmoil of the first half of the 20th century, banking crises under Bretton Woods were virtually non-existent.

This economic serenity would last until 1971, when the US abandoned the gold standard, and the Bretton Woods system collapsed.

Why did the US abandon the gold standard? During the 1960s, the US had spent significantly on its Great Society program and the Vietnam War. Sure enough, much of this spending was funded by increasing their money supply, and by 1971, there were many more dollars in circulation without a corresponding increase in the gold reserves held. The president at the time, Richard Nixon, started re-valuing the dollar's pegged rate to gold downwards.

A crisis of confidence ensued, as nations tried to convert their dollars to physical gold, fearing that there weren't sufficient reserves to back the dollars at their pegged rate. At this point, Nixon felt there was no other option but to suspend the convertibility of dollars to gold altogether and the Bretton Woods system was effectively ended.

Stock-To-Flow

Why did gold become the de facto currency of choice as money developed in its early days? Was it the shiniest metal available? Or did early leaders just love the color and feel of it?

Not quite. Gold has become known as one of the world's most durable metals. It is stable. It does not burst into flames. It does not dissipate into the atmosphere or corrode away over time. It can be handled and it does not wear down excessively, nor does it poison those who hold it. It is very difficult to destroy.

However, it is possible to melt it down and mint coins from it. These properties make gold practically suited for use as a currency, as it can handle the demands of being circulated and handled by many people throughout society.

But there are other precious metals that would fit the bill. Silver is a good example of a metal that is very practically suited to being currency, as is bronze. Indeed, both these metals were also used as currency in many civilizations, usually as lower value coins compared to the gold coins.

Gold comes out on top for one reason; scarcity. Gold struck the sweet spot between abundance and scarcity. It was abundant enough that it could be mined in sufficient volume to satisfy the monetary needs of the time, but it was scarce enough that it was a fantastic store of value because it was very difficult to mine significantly more.

That last point is key. Gold is rare, yes, however around 3,000 tons of gold are mined each year. That's a lot of gold! But proportionally, it is less than 2% of all the gold that currently exists.

This property can be expressed through a ratio known as stock-to-flow. That sounds quite fancy but it's actually very simple.

Stock is the amount of a commodity that is already held in inventories, effectively, the total amount of it that exists.

Flow is the amount of that same commodity that is produced in one year.

The total amount of gold ever mined is approximately 190,000 tons, whilst annual production is circa 3,000 tons. Taking the 190,000 tons divided by 3,000 tons, we calculate a stock-to-flow ratio of 63. It means it would take 63 years at current production rates to double the current gold stock. Other metals do not score anywhere near as highly, for example, silver comes in at a ratio of 22.

Gold scores very highly because the level of stock is so high, hundreds of thousands of tons have been mined over the years and it is virtually impossible to destroy. The flow, meanwhile, is very difficult to increase due to the difficulty of finding and extracting gold, particularly when trying to do so cost-effectively.

Why are commodities with a high stock-to-flow ratio considered good money? Quite simply, because they hold their worth, they are a good store of value. Why? Because it is very difficult to drastically increase new supply of the commodity.

Let's look at an example. Let's take a different metal such as platinum, which has a low stock-to-flow ratio around 1. That means for every ton mined there exists 1 ton held in reserves already. If we assume all the platinum mined in any given year is used for industrial purposes, the stock-to-flow ratio would remain unchanged, and given the stable supply and demand you could reasonably expect the price of platinum to stay constant.

Now let's say a new use of platinum is discovered which triggers a spike in demand. In the short-term, this will likely lead to a price rise. However, higher prices will attract more miners to the market. As more miners join, the production of platinum increases, and the available supply increases which will bring the price back down.

Conversely, let's say there is a reduction in the demand for platinum. Less demand will result in a surplus of supply and the price will likely fall. Falling prices will cause miners to cut costs and reduce production, which lowers the available supply and the price stabilizes.

Commodities with a low stock-to-flow ratio are therefore susceptible to bubbles and collapses in price. Not ideal for storing your life savings.

Gold is not immune to price swings, it is still susceptible to significant changes in demand but its high stock-to-flow gives it price stability and a strong resolve against these significant price fluctuations.

So what has all this got to do with bitcoin? At the time of writing, Bitcoin has just been through its third halving. Every time the block rewards are halved, the stock-to-flow ratio of bitcoin more than doubles, as the expected flow each year is significantly reduced. Following the third halving, bitcoin has a stock-to-flow ratio of 56, almost on par with gold.

This means bitcoin should hold its value resolutely and become less susceptible to price bubbles as time goes on. Whether or not valuations for the future bitcoin price can be derived from its stock-to-flow ratio is currently a hot topic of debate in the cryptocurrency community.

The Fiat Era

End of the Gold Standard

Firstly, no we are not talking about Fiat, the Italian car manufacturer here. The term "fiat" comes from Latin and literally translates as the decree "Let it be done". In economic terms, a fiat currency is one that does not have any intrinsic value, it is backed only by the government. There is no precious asset such as gold for which the currency can be redeemed.

Ever since the US abolished the convertibility of dollars to gold in 1971 and thus effectively ended the gold standard, the world has entered a brave new era of fiat currencies. Dollars, euros, sterling, yen, rupees, the lot. They all now "float" against each other without any of them being tied to any form of solid backing.

Why is a dollar still worth a dollar? Because everyone agrees a dollar is a dollar. A dollar can no longer be exchanged for a set amount of gold, but you can still buy real things with them because everyone is willing to accept them. What other choice do you have?

In principle then, this system sounds plausible. But it requires a lot of trust and a lot of faith that those in power know what they are doing with the money supply. Without a commodity backing every note, governments are free to tinker with the amount of currency circulating under their control.

This has paved the way for economists to push all manner of complicated economic theories, that they could somehow control the economy through manipulation of interest rates, spending, and the money supply. We've all seen how that has turned out as we've lurched from crisis to crisis over the past 50 years.

Under the gold standard, every currency note effectively represented a small piece of gold. This meant that a country doing well and exporting lots of goods would build up its gold reserves as it sold goods to other nations. It would run a trade surplus; more money coming in than going out.

This build-up of gold reserves would mean there is more money circulating in that country, as every gram of gold would be accounted for by a paper note of some sort. This would have the effect of pushing up prices as there is more money compared to the real value of goods and services in that country.

As domestic prices increase, imports from other countries begin to look more attractive. A subsequent increase in imports, then results in more gold flowing out of the country. If more gold flows out than in, that country is now running a trade deficit. As money flows out, gold reserves decline and domestic prices reduce, leading to more exports. The cycle repeats.

Using hard money like gold, this pattern would self-correct and it would be difficult for any country to run up either a huge surplus or a huge deficit. However, under a fiat system, the same rules do not apply and governments can operate with large deficits to fund their spending. As a result, levels of government debt have spiraled out of control over the past 50 years.

Easy money reigns as central banks believe they can stimulate spending to keep the economy growing. Exactly what that spending is, isn't too much of a concern. This has allowed governments to run up massive deficits as they borrow more and more, using more borrowing to repay existing debt holders.

Now, anyone with any common sense can see that borrowing more to pay off your debts is not a sustainable way of operating. Certainly, individuals or businesses would not be able to operate by continually taking on more credit to pay off existing debt. Do you think your bank would continue giving you a greater credit limit on your credit card each year if you never paid off the balance? Of course not. Normal people are on the hook, as you would expect. Banks need their loans repaying to successfully operate, so this is only fair.

But when it comes to governments, the same rules do not apply. The immortal nature of a government means debt can just be rolled over time and time again. Ultimately, some nations do default, Argentina being a good example of a nation that has defaulted on their obligations many times, but generally speaking, they have been allowed to run up ever-increasing debt without any real means of generating the funds to pay it down.

All they can do is try and raise additional revenues through taxes. But the tax hikes would have to be so severe that it would cripple the growth of the economy, which has been falsely stimulated through excessive borrowing for decades. No politician would stay in office long if they reduced public spending and hiked taxes at the same time. And that is what it would take to bring these colossal deficits under control.

It is no wonder that term after term, politicians have kicked this can down the road and continued to borrow to fund spending. We are now so far down that road that no politician would get anywhere near office if they dared to deviate from that course.

The immediate impact of fiat currency was clear to see in the 1970s. Overly expansive monetary policy in the US resulted in huge growth in the money supply and rampant inflation, in an episode that became known as the "Great Inflation". It took years of monetary tightening to bring inflation under control. The primary method economists used was to raise interest rates.

Interest Rates

Interest rates are effectively the cost of money. Money has a value just like everything else. When money is in high demand, you would expect interest rates to be higher. After all, there is only so much money to go around so if there's a lot of demand, banks can charge a higher rate because there will be someone willing to pay it.

In conjunction with the lending, a higher rate encourages people to save money, supplying the banks with the funds they need to then lend out to borrowers. Conversely, lower interest rates should accompany times when money is not in such high demand, for example, an economic downturn. Central banks' favorite trick is to lower interest rates to boost the economy and stimulate growth.

How does this work? Lower rates encourage borrowers to borrow and spend or invest more. It has the twin effect of making saving less attractive, so people are more inclined to spend. Why not splash out on that holiday if your money would otherwise be earning next to nothing in the bank?

By this logic, you would expect the levels of debt to be lower when interest rates are low. There is less demand for money, less debt, therefore a lower rate should entice people to borrow. Similarly, during times of high interest rates, you would expect levels of debt to be higher. Fundamentally, because there is more demand for money.

However, after 50 years of central bank manipulation and tinkering, we find ourselves in a situation where interest rates are effectively 0%. They cannot go lower unless they go negative, which they could by the way. With such low interest rates, you would expect very low levels of debt; if they are having to loan money interest-free there *really* must be no demand for it.

However, we have the opposite. There are record levels of debt in economies around the globe. US national debt is now over $26 trillion. Yes, you read that right, not $26 billion, but $26 trillion!

Quantitative Easing and Modern Economies

The wheels nearly fell off the careering debt juggernaut in 2008 during the financial crisis. This is a whole other story which we won't go into here, however, one of the outcomes of that crisis was something called quantitative easing.

That sounds suitably complicated. It is, in fact, just a disguised way of saying money printing. In order to keep the global economy from total collapse, central banks had to step in and buy government bonds directly. These bonds would normally be sold to investors, pension funds and the like, and are the governments' primary method of borrowing.

Now, to pay for these bonds, central banks simply print more money. Or these days, they just create an additional balance on their ledger. After all, it would logistically be quite difficult to physically print trillions of dollars! This precedent has continued during the current global pandemic crisis. Quantitative easing like we have never seen has been authorized by countries the world over to try and avoid a complete economic meltdown.

Why is this needed? It's a complicated subject, but put simply, through years of access to easy money and cheap loans, corporations have become more and more highly levered; they have more debt and fewer reserves. Any sort of economic downturn and they are suddenly exposed as they simply do not have the cash reserves to cover themselves during the barren period.

Many large corporations have exacerbated the situation by spending all their spare cash on share buybacks. This is an accounting trick where they buy back their own shares. It is a way of manipulating key performance indicators such as earnings *per share* because those shares are taken out of circulation. This usually has the desired impact of increasing the share price.

However, in times of need, they are now short of cash

and require government intervention, or even a bailout to be able to continue operating. And at present, the bailouts keep coming. We are seeing financial stimulus unlike anything the world has ever known. At the time of writing, trillions and trillions of dollars have been promised and printed to keep the global money-go-round spinning.

But surely it is a good thing to save these businesses from bankruptcy? Well, not necessarily. Free market economies are built upon the premise of creating value. Companies that cannot do this go out of business and those resources are re-used elsewhere in a more profitable venture.

Through constant stimulus and low interest rates, many businesses have been able to continue operating that would have otherwise gone under. The cheap loans available enable them to pay their overheads and interest charges, but they are unable to repay any capital of the loan. In an economy where interest rates were priced fairly, there's no way they could survive being charged a higher rate. These businesses are known as zombies.

The problem with zombies is that they consume resources that could otherwise be invested more effectively. They have no chance of spurring economic growth because they are simply treading water. When an economic downturn comes along, they are in grave danger of bankruptcy. Unless of course, they employ so many people that they are considered "too big to fail". In which case, there will be immense pressure on the government to bail them out. This was the case with some of the big banks in 2008 during the financial crisis.

With enough of these zombie companies, you can find yourself with a whole zombie economy. Whilst it may be seen as a good thing to maintain zombies to preserve jobs in the short-term, funding this type of inefficient business actually hinders job creation in the longer term, as those resources are not being put to their best use. They are not creating real value.

Why then, are they allowed to continue operating? Why aren't they allowed to fail? The simple answer is that there are too many people with vested interests in keeping them afloat. Whilst long-term prospects for these businesses may be bleak, they are still capable of making short-term profits. And it is the drive for these short-term profits which exaggerates the problem further.

As we have seen with share buybacks, some CEOs are quite happy to engage in practices that boost the short-term share price at the detriment of longer-term sustainability. They may also be prepared to prioritize short-term profits at the expense of the longer-term health of the business. Why? Usually, because their pay is linked in some way to either the share price, or profit levels.

We see the same short-termism within politics. No politician is thinking further ahead than the next four years. They are more concerned with short-term GDP growth as this is generally accepted as the sign of a healthy economy. Whether that growth actually benefits society or the environment is usually a secondary consideration.

In the UK, online and offline gambling is booming.

The economy loves this because it translates into lots of GDP. Given high GDP growth, the politicians will tell us the economy is great and everyone is becoming better off. But is this really benefitting society? The majority of players lose money and the most frequent visitors to betting shops are the poor; dreaming of a big win but more likely to lose the money they desperately need to put food on the table. What does this say about the current state of modern money? People feel so desperate that instead of buying food, they would rather chance their arm on a spin of the wheel, in the hope of striking it lucky.

Nowadays, we have more people than ever needing to visit food banks to feed themselves, yet simultaneously we also have more billionaires than ever before. How have we reached a point where the polarization of rich and poor has grown to such epic proportions?

Impacts of Inflation

The impact of newly created money and subsequent inflation in an economy can be nicely summarized by a phenomenon known as the Cantillon effect, named after the 18th-century economist Richard Cantillon who devised it.

Simply put, this theory denotes that any expansion in the money supply does not impact prices evenly. Think of it like a spoonful of honey being dropped into a cup. Initially, it will blob together in the middle and then over time, it will spread to cover the base of the cup. In monetary terms, those closest to the new money stand to gain the most. Prices will increase for everyone, but the poorest (those near the edge of the cup) are the last to receive any of this new money.

Those near the source of the money, usually big corporations and banks, can use the money to invest for their own gain. Eventually, that money will filter down to the average guy on the street but not before everyone before him has taken their cut. It has never been more apparent than in the current spate of pandemic related bailouts. Yes, some countries are paying money directly to individuals but this pales in comparison to the level of funds being distributed to large corporations. Small and medium-sized businesses are also struggling to get hold of the funding they need to continue operating.

In a nutshell, the Cantillon effect suggests that money doesn't flow evenly. In modern economies, the vast majority of new money goes first to the rich and powerful, who benefit most from it. The effect of all this, is that the rich grow richer and the poor grow poorer. With the money supply increasing significantly since the end of the gold standard in 1971, it is no surprise that inequality has continued to accelerate dramatically over the past 50 years.

Inflation then, which normally results from an increase in the money supply, is effectively a stealth tax moving money to the rich. The rich and powerful benefit from the new money created, while everyone else is worse off through increased price levels and diminished purchasing power.

The purchasing power of $1 today is the approximate equivalent of 15 cents in 1971. That means you need six times as many dollars to buy the same cup of coffee today.

Here is a short summary of some of the other effects that have manifested during the fiat era:

- All major currencies have depreciated against gold.

- US National debt increased from $398 billion in 1971 to over $26 trillion in 2020.

- There have been over 40 documented cases of hyperinflation around the globe since 1971. Between 1950-1970 there were none.

- In 1971, CEOs of the 350 largest US firms earned on average 22 times the average worker's salary, in 2018 they earned 278 times the average worker.

- The US federal minimum wage in 1971 was $1.60, equivalent to $10.13 in 2020 dollars. The federal minimum wage in 2020 is $7.25, a significant reduction in real purchasing power.

- In the UK the average house price was 2.6 times average earnings in 1971. By 2019, it was 8.4 times average earnings.

- The percentage of 25-29 year-olds in the US living with parents or grandparents doubled from under 15% in 1971 to over 30% by 2015.

- The amount of disposable income saved by individuals in the US fell from 13.2% in 1970 to 7.6% in 2019, having been as low as 3.6% before the financial crisis in 2008.

Of course, many of these statistics are influenced by a host of different factors, however, the dramatic nature of the changes since moving into a fiat world is undeniable.

Many people can sense that something is wrong. Even if they can't put their finger on exactly what that is, they know. They see the inequality on the streets. They see the welfare cuts. They see the environmental damage. They see the excessive consumption of the rich. They see the rampant greed on Wall Street.

It is no surprise that we now have routine protests such as Occupy Wall Street and the Gilets Jaunes on the streets of Paris. People are starting to rebel. The problem is, those in power have direct access to the source of all the new money; central banks. Governments are the ones who benefit the most from this arrangement. So how do you go about relinquishing that control from them?

The Bitcoin Era?

"I don't believe we shall ever have a good money again before we take the thing out of the hands of government, that is, we can't take it violently out of the hands of government, all we can do is by some sly roundabout way introduce something that they can't stop."

- *Friedrich A. Hayek, economist, and advocate of Austrian economics*

Let's take a step back. At the start of this chapter, we asked why do we need Bitcoin? After all, digital payments have been around for a long time.

Now that we have explored some of the issues with the current fiat monetary system, it should be clear that this system is ultimately destined to fail. We now live in a world where there is more money than ever.

Central banks are printing fresh cash at breakneck speeds to try and keep the fiat credit bubble from deflating. This can only go on for so long. You simply cannot solve a debt problem by creating more and more debt.

So what would a solution to these issues look like? A move back to the gold standard? Or could bitcoin become a global currency?

To answer that question, let's look at the key characteristics of effective money and compare the merits of fiat, gold, and bitcoin for each.

Limited Supply

Bitcoin differs from fiat currency in many ways but perhaps the most important difference is that of scarcity. Bitcoin's total supply is capped at 21 million. There are currently less than 21 million in circulation, but there can never be more than 21 million. It is written into Bitcoin's code that the supply is capped; finite.

On the other end of the spectrum, fiat currency is uncapped, and the total supply is increasing at a faster rate than ever before.

As we have seen with the example of gold, a scarce asset holds its value well, and provides a robust form of money, while assets that are easily produced in vast quantities tend to lose value quite rapidly.

This particular property of bitcoin is one of its main attractions. Bitcoin is an emerging new technology, it is becoming more and more well known by the day and more people are starting to take an interest. This interest usually translates into more demand. More demand for an asset with a limited supply pushes the price up through simple laws of supply and demand.

Bitcoin cannot be beaten when it comes to limited supply. Yes, gold is also mined in limited amounts each year as we have seen when looking at stock-to-flow, however, who's to say a massive new gold reserve won't be found somewhere under the Earth's surface? It's also quite possible that huge amounts of gold could be found in space, on asteroids or other celestial objects.

Any such discovery, albeit a remote chance at best, could send the price of gold tumbling as huge amounts of new supply are introduced. With bitcoin that is simply not possible, as future supply changes are already coded and set in stone until the maximum supply of 21 million is reached around the year 2140.

We can all agree that it is not even worth entertaining a comparison with fiat currency when it comes to limited supply.

Durability

To be effective money, a currency must be durable; it must be hardy enough to not degrade or deteriorate to the detriment of its value.

Paper notes aren't the most durable item in the world but they can be replaced at banks, and of course, there are now many options to pay digitally for items with debit and credit cards or even your smartphone. The digital age has made durability much less of an important issue when it comes to money in the modern world.

That said, physical cash is easily destroyed. Gold less so. Bitcoin even less so. Being a digital asset bitcoin cannot be destroyed. It can be lost if you lose your private keys, but when it comes to being durable, again it cannot be beaten.

The topic of durability raises another important issue; custody. It is worth noting that if you have your money in a bank account it may be safe from physical damage or deterioration, but you do not have physical ownership of that cash. Effectively, you have an IOU from the bank to say that they will give you that sum of cash on demand. If there was a run on the bank and everyone requested all their money at the same time, thanks to fractional reserve banking, the bank would not be able to pay everyone.

In such a scenario you could fall back on your government who may guarantee a certain amount but that's not really a situation in which you want to find yourself.

Similarly, if you hold gold through a third party, you only have an IOU to your gold. You are reliant upon the third party to honor that IOU should you want to take delivery. Of course, you may think it is unlikely you will ever find yourself in such a situation, but it is something worth thinking about.

You could keep your supply of cash and gold in a secure deposit box if you wanted physical ownership of it, but that comes with additional cost and the inconvenience of access every time you wanted to save or spend.

With bitcoin, however, you can hold your wealth in a wallet, be it online or offline. You have ownership of your own money and are not reliant on any third party for access, to send or receive. This may seem like a trivial difference to current online banking, however, in countries where rogue governments may seize assets, this is *incredibly* important.

When you have your wealth stored with a third party, it can very easily be frozen or seized by the authorities. If you are lucky enough to live in a democratic civilized country this is unlikely to keep you awake at night, but if you lived somewhere under tyrannical rule, this could be a significant problem.

With your wealth stored securely in a bitcoin wallet, it cannot be seized. We'll talk more about why this is so important shortly.

Third-party custody is, of course, not necessarily a bad thing. Many people are simply not prepared or equipped to hold all of their own money. In fact, virtually no-one does. Having money stored in a bank gives us peace of mind and reduces our risk. Any fraudulent transactions can usually be traced or reversed, or at worst the bank will reimburse you from their exorbitant profits.

Portability

Going hand in hand with the custody issue is the characteristic of portability, or in other words, how easily the money can be moved.

Fiat and paper money scores reasonably well here. Cash is lightweight and easy to transport in small amounts, and we now have digital payments that enable us to send money around the world quickly, to anyone who has a bank account. Which, by the way, isn't everyone. But we'll talk about that in a moment.

To send your fiat you do of course need a bank or a payment transactor, and they don't work for free. You may be able to send personal payments free of charge but the banks certainly do alright from their charges to corporations, and individuals sending large sums.

Gold fails miserably when it comes to portability. A heavy precious metal is probably one of the most difficult things you can transfer to another individual on the other side of the world. It is slow and expensive, to say the least.

Bitcoin excels in portability. Particularly now that the Lightning Network is being developed, sums of any amount can be sent rapidly for minimal cost. Even large on-chain transactions are quicker and cheaper than using a bank. For example, in April 2020, 146,500 bitcoin were moved in a single transaction. At the time that was equivalent to around $1bn. And the fee for moving such a huge sum? Less than 0.0001 bitcoin. Or about $0.70. Banks simply cannot compete with that.

Divisibility

To be an effective currency, any unit of account must be divisible into small enough chunks that it can be used easily for purchases.

Fiat currency usually works absolutely fine in this respect as most currencies are divisible into dollars and cents for example. There isn't much that you would want to buy costing less than one cent so this works perfectly adequately in practice.

This is another area where gold struggles badly. Using the example of dollars and cents, historically many countries would use gold coins for dollars and coins of lower value such as silver to represent cents. Gold itself is not easily divided without the significant effort of melting down and re-minting coins. Of course, this problem can be avoided by using a paper currency linked to the value of gold, as we saw under the Bretton Woods system.

Bitcoin is extremely divisible as each bitcoin can be divided into 100 million smaller denominations known as sats, after the founder Satoshi Nakamoto.

At current value, that puts each sat at much much less than 1 cent in US dollar terms. If the value of all bitcoin rose to the same level as the current supply of all dollars in the US, each sat would be worth almost 1 cent. And each bitcoin would be worth nearly $1 million.

Uniformity

For ease of use, you would expect each unit of your money to be the same. Every dollar bill is printed in exactly the same design, in exactly the same way on exactly the same paper. They may have unique serial numbers but to all intents and purposes they are identical.

Similarly, when gold was used to mint coins they would be created identically. These days, most gold stored in reserves is separated into bars of identical weight. One drawback of gold in this respect is that there are different purities of gold, with 24 karat gold being the purest. One gold bar may not be the equal of another then, and it requires some form of verification or testing to ensure that it is in its purest form.

With bitcoin being a digital asset, it does not have a physical representation or form, but being digital gives it perfect uniformity as every bitcoin is mined in the same way and has the exact same form.

Acceptability

You may have the most exceptional form of money but if no-one will accept it for goods or services it is useless.

Almost by default fiat currencies win hands down here. A government-backed currency which is written into law as legal tender has to be accepted by everyone in that jurisdiction. Many merchants would also go as far as to accept other national currencies as well as their own. Indeed, for businesses, this can be an effective way to protect themselves against exchange rate fluctuations.

At present, gold fails in this respect as it is not used widely for paying for goods and services. It does, however, still hold value, therefore, a Bretton Woods style system with fiat values tied to gold would still be possible and would probably still work quite effectively.

This is also the one area where bitcoin *currently* really struggles. Yes, a small smattering of merchants are starting to accept bitcoin payments and this is increasing all the time, but at the moment adoption is simply not high enough for bitcoin to be considered a viable currency by many.

However, rapid advances are being made in this area. Even if merchant adoption is slow, many companies are now developing Visa and Mastercard debit cards that can be linked to a cryptocurrency wallet.

In theory, if you wanted to keep all your money in bitcoin and spend it via one of these cards you could do so.

This is something that simply would not have been possible just a few years ago, so acceptability is improving all the time.

Bitcoin As A Store Of Value

You may have noticed that people in Bitcoin circles are generally not that interested in spending their bitcoin. Quite the opposite in fact. Many are more interested in accumulating and holding their bitcoin. Why is this?

Well, look at any bitcoin chart and that will become quite obvious. This is an asset that has been on a non-stop increase in value ever since it was created in 2009. There have been significant drawdowns along the way, known as "bear markets", where the price trends downwards for a period, but overall the trajectory has been one way and that way is up.

Bitcoin Pizza Day is celebrated by many bitcoin enthusiasts each year on 22nd May. This is to commemorate the first documented physical purchase made using bitcoin, when Laszlo Hanyecz purchased two Papa John's pizzas on May 22nd, 2010.

The two pizzas cost 10,000 bitcoin, which at the time was a modest $41. In December 2017 bitcoin prices, those two pizzas cost the equivalent of $100 million each!

Those pizzas valued bitcoin at $0.004 each. Less than half a cent. At its peak in 2017, one bitcoin was worth just under $20,000. One dollar invested in bitcoin in May 2010 would have been worth an eye-watering $5 million at the 2017 peak.

Now can you see why people are reluctant to spend

their bitcoin?!

You may have seen the acronym "HODL" used widely by those in the Bitcoin community. While also being a nice play on the word "hold", this stands for "Hold On for Dear Life". This epitomizes the attitude of many bitcoin owners; huge gains are possible but it is a roller coaster ride.

The major peaks in the bitcoin price over the last 10 years have all been accompanied by crashes of over 80%, which, compared to traditional financial markets, makes bitcoin one of the most volatile and risky things you can invest in. But, risk and reward go hand in hand when it comes to investing, so it is no surprise that an asset that could potentially appreciate many times over also comes with significant risk.

Of course, the magnitude of the *astronomical* gains highlighted above are unlikely to be made again. In the early days, Bitcoin was more of an experiment than anything else and its chances of avoiding failure were considered quite slim. In fact, Bitcoin has been declared "dead" over 350 times in the mainstream media, but to this day the network continues to produce block after block just as designed.

These days bitcoin is gaining wider and wider acceptance as a financial instrument. Through brokers, it now trades on some of the largest exchanges in the world. Far from being a techie experiment, it is now very much in the mainstream and is primarily seen by many as a store of value.

Historically the price of bitcoin has only gone up.

Now, many individual and institutional investors are starting to see it as a good option to store their wealth to protect it from the ever-increasing inflation of fiat money supplies.

When talking about a store of value, gold is typically seen as the best example. During times of crisis, investors flock towards gold because this is seen as the ultimate hard money for the reasons discussed previously. Following the 2008 financial crisis, the price of gold more than doubled before hitting a peak in 2011.

Why did this happen? As stock and real estate prices crashed, investors flocked to move their money somewhere where it would be safe, into what's known as a "safe haven" asset. That asset was gold. The supply of gold is relatively fixed due to its high stock-to-flow ratio, therefore, the price increased dramatically as demand vastly outstripped supply.

Gold is very good when it comes to protecting wealth, but in times of normal economic growth, it doesn't usually provide a very high return. Therefore, once the global economy recovered, money started flowing back out of gold into other assets offering higher returns such as stocks.

Bitcoin has long been described as potential "Digital Gold" due to its similarities with physical gold, in that both have a limited supply and low level of inflation. And it is for this reason, that many people are investing in bitcoin today, and why many of those investors are reluctant to sell.

Holding bitcoin is seen as a way to protect against

the rampant increases in fiat money supply and the reduction in purchasing power that follows through inflation. As an investment, there is considerable risk; Bitcoin could still fail. But it has survived its first decade; its hardest decade. All things considered, if it was going to fail you would think it would have done so by now. But it continues to be resilient to everything thrown at it and the network just continues growing stronger.

Many investors are starting to see bitcoin as a considerable asymmetric trade. That means, the potential upside vastly outweighs the downside. Yes, Bitcoin could fail and the price could go to zero. In such a scenario any money invested would be lost, you would be down 100%. But this is an asset which could conceivably, in time, go to $1 million per bitcoin. It sounds ridiculous but it is within the realms of possibility. After all, when bitcoin used to trade for $1 or $2 per bitcoin, everyone thought a price of $20,000 per bitcoin was inconceivable.

From the price at the time of writing, an increase to $1 million per bitcoin would yield a return of over 11,000%, or over 100 times the original investment! So the trade has a potential downside of 100% and a potential upside of 11,000% or more. When looking at it in these terms, it is clear to see why many investors are interested in putting at least some money into bitcoin.

Bitcoin is in a spot where it has not yet become large enough to really be considered a "safe haven" asset. If an asset routinely drops over 80%, that certainly doesn't seem like a *safe* place to store your life savings. To give some perspective, the total market capitalization, that is, the total value of all bitcoin in circulation at current price, is around $120 billion at the time of writing. That may sound like a lot but by comparison, the total market capitalization of gold is currently $9 trillion, 75 times the market capitalization of bitcoin.

This is the reason bitcoin is so volatile. In terms of financial assets, it is still very small. Therefore, if significant sums of money flow into or out of bitcoin, it can result in wild price fluctuations. Think of it as a body of water. If you throw a bucket of water into a half-full bathtub, that new water will send waves all around the tub. Throw it into a large garden pond and you will still see some waves but they will flatten out by the time they reach the edges. Throw it into a huge lake and there will barely be much of a ripple.

The one thing common to all three, however, is that the water level rises each time. The bigger the body of water, the more buckets you need to throw in to see a significant rise. Gold is like the lake in our example, it would take huge amounts of new money to flow in, to make a significant impact on price. Bitcoin is probably somewhere between the bathtub and the pond at present. The price still fluctuates significantly when money flows in and out.

This volatility is another reason why bitcoin is impractical for use as a currency right now. If goods were priced in bitcoin you might find your groceries costing 10% more or less than they did just a week ago. Over long time periods, the price could fluctuate by significantly more than that. No-one in their right mind would choose to use such a currency.

But what about those people who don't have a choice?

Bitcoin In The Developing World

Even today, many people find themselves in a situation where they have no choice but to use a currency that is wildly fluctuating. Unfortunately, in the majority of these cases, the currency is usually depreciating rapidly. We are talking now about hyperinflation.

At the time of writing, there is ongoing hyperinflation in Lebanon, and in Venezuela, where it has been an issue for several years. The people in these countries have no choice but to see their money, their life savings, lose value rapidly as the price of goods and services skyrocket.

This is not a new phenomenon, and as discussed earlier, in the post-Bretton Woods world it is more prevalent than ever.

What has this got to do with Bitcoin? Well, previously these poor people seeing their savings go up in smoke could do very little about it. The government issues a national currency and everyone is forced to use it. Conceivably you could try and convert your money into a more stable currency, such as US dollars, to protect against the hyperinflation, however, the government may also exercise controls over the transfer of foreign currencies. Or nations such as the US may impose sanctions that would prohibit the exchange of dollars.

But now with bitcoin, they have an option. To buy bitcoin, all you need is an internet connection and that bitcoin can then be held securely in a wallet. You are still at the mercy of volatile swings in the bitcoin price, but when faced with hyperinflation, this is a risk many would be willing to take. Bitcoin can also serve as a gateway. While it may not be possible to transfer their home currency directly to US dollars, by using bitcoin people can circumvent any such controls.

Their home currency is converted to bitcoin, then that bitcoin is converted to US dollars which can be held in an offshore account. This is already happening extensively in South America. The volume of bitcoin traded in both Venezuela and Argentina is skyrocketing as people seek out ways to protect their wealth, faced with devastating hyperinflation, dysfunctional economies, and governments on the brink of default.

Taking this a step further, Bitcoin's decentralized nature means those moving countries or seeking asylum, could simply take their bitcoin with them. Bitcoin can be left in an online wallet, it doesn't need to be physically transferred with the person. Provided they have a means of safely storing their private keys, which could also be done online, there is no physical item that could be confiscated to stop them from moving their wealth through borders. It is also quite possible to memorize a wallet seed phrase, making bitcoin completely non-confiscatable.

As you probably know, if you turned up at the airport with a suitcase full of your life savings, be it cash or gold bars, customs might just take an interest!

The ease with which bitcoin can be accessed creates another exciting use case for the cryptocurrency. It is estimated that 1.7 billion adults around the world remain "unbanked"; they have no account with a bank or financial institution. Why is this the case? Opening a bank account isn't the easiest thing to do, it turns out. You need a government-issued ID, proof of fixed address, and a clear credit history as a minimum in many countries.

This immediately rules out anyone who is homeless and countless others. These people are forced to transact mainly in cash, and usually incur higher costs as a result of using check-cashing businesses, prepaid cards, and money transfer services.

The number of unbanked is much higher in poorer and developing nations, but that's not to say it's a third world problem. There remain millions of people without bank accounts in developed countries such as the US and the UK.

With bitcoin, these people have an alternative. With just a basic smartphone they could install a mobile wallet which would enable them to access a form of money that can be sent round the world cheaply and easily. This would effectively give them access to all the benefits of a bank account, without needing a third-party institution. Many people who already have bank accounts would probably also see the advantages of such a system!

While we are talking about bitcoin here, it should be noted that many other cryptocurrencies could fulfill this purpose. One you may have heard of is Libra, the cryptocurrency being developed by Facebook. Libra will have the advantage of already having billions of people signed up to their network. If wallets can be linked to Facebook accounts, this will rapidly increase adoption of Libra and in terms of "banking the unbanked", Libra will likely take the lead on this ahead of bitcoin.

So if Libra is better than bitcoin at this, why do we still need bitcoin? Two main reasons. Firstly, Libra will be under some form of centralized control, therefore, it will be confiscatable by a central authority. Secondly, Libra will be pegged to fiat currencies, therefore, as a store of value, it has all the same issues that plague fiat currencies as discussed earlier.

Cryptocurrencies such as Libra could be adopted quite rapidly, they are essentially crypto-dollars. Bitcoin is more like crypto-gold, a sound money that will hold its value much better over time. For the same reason people move funds out of fiat currencies into bitcoin, they will also move funds out of other cryptocurrencies into bitcoin.

Deflation By Design

Let's say Bitcoin continues to gather more and more momentum and adoption continues to increase over time, as it has done for the past 10 years. Let's say one day it does grow to such a size that it becomes a global reserve currency, accepted all around the world.

What would this future look like?

Well, firstly, as discussed the price of one bitcoin would swell to an enormous sum in dollar terms. One bitcoin would probably be worth in excess of $1 million. In such a scenario, bitcoin could replace the US dollar as the world's reserve currency, so it may not even make sense to derive such a valuation. Alternatively, this future vision could take the form of a new Bretton Woods system where bitcoin is the underlying asset that all currencies are pegged to.

Either way, the global economy would operate in a radically different way. With the current fiat system, inflation reigns supreme. Central banks and governments target a small amount of inflation each year to encourage spending. If your money is losing value each year, there is more of an incentive to spend. Lots of spending results in higher GDP, which is the yardstick by which all economies are measured. GDP growth is seen as the holy grail that shows an economy is functioning well; bringing greater prosperity to all those who reside in that country.

Except, as we have seen, that isn't the case. Gambling

companies and casinos being a great example. They can significantly boost GDP but are they really adding anything to society? We are told repeatedly that the stock markets are doing great so the economy must be doing great. Except, the stock markets are not the economy. The stock markets are not reflecting the reality of what is going on out there in the real world. We have a disconnect.

What inflation means for the average person, is that they need a pay rise every year, just to keep pace with the price increases in all the goods that they buy. Inflation is usually measured by the Consumer Price Index (CPI), which takes a basket of goods and services typically consumed by the average person and measures the change in the weighted average price of those items from year to year.

Typically, governments target CPI growth, or inflation, of 2% per annum. So you need a 2% pay rise each year to keep pace with the rate at which everything you buy is getting more expensive. That's not ideal, but also 2% doesn't sound like too much, right? Well, here's the thing, CPI doesn't include any measures to do with house prices. What we have seen over the past 50 years, is that growth, or inflation, in house prices has dramatically outstripped the official rate of inflation as calculated through CPI.

This is clearly demonstrated by the fact that average house prices have drastically increased as a multiple of average earnings. The average pay rise each year simply cannot keep up with the growth in real estate prices. Why has this happened? Through the Cantillon effect, new money finds its way to the rich and powerful, and they see property as a good place to invest it. Take London for example, many penthouse super-apartments lie unoccupied for long periods, while those who own them reside elsewhere at another of their properties. They are an investment.

Properties of the super-rich in London may seem a long way from the average guy on the street, but that money flows somewhere. Whoever sold that property may then invest the funds in other properties and the chain continues, but it is those who already owned the assets that are benefitting most.

The vast sums of money printed in the last 15 years would result in catastrophic inflation if that money went straight into circulation for the general public to spend. The reason we don't have high inflation is because it is siphoned off at every level and invested in other assets such as real estate and stocks. This is also the reason why we see asset bubbles forming.

All the while, governments continue to tell us that inflation is a good thing, a sign of a growing economy, a sign that everyone must be getting more prosperous. It is, in fact, the opposite. The rich continue to grow richer and the poor continue to grow poorer.

Now, if we ignore everything we already know about inflation, does this continual price increase actually make any sense?

Technological advances over the last 50 years have generated an untold number of efficiencies and savings in all areas of our lives. Resources are being used more effectively than ever before.

Take for example, the music business. Many years ago, if you wanted to listen to music your options were the radio or a vinyl record. You would need a record player and the vinyl, which might have 3 or 4 songs at most, and all this would not be cheap to buy. Then we had cassettes which could hold a bit more music, followed by CDs and finally, we went fully digital with MP3s.

At each stage of this progression, you could get a little bit more music for your money. Nowadays, you don't even need MP3s, you can stream a choice of millions of tracks for a very low monthly cost. You even have many different streaming services to choose from, some of which might be bundled with other offerings such as TV or broadband packages.

By definition, this is the opposite of inflationary. With each progression, your money will get you more than before. This is *deflationary*. And this is undoubtedly a good thing.

There are countless examples where technology has improved our lives in this way. The best example is most probably the smartphone. With one device that can be obtained for a relatively low monthly fee, there are thousands of functions that would have previously required significant expense and time commitments to perform.

You no longer need a GPS. You no longer need a digital camera. You can video call friends and family around the world instantly and for no additional charge. You can order shopping at the touch of a button and have it delivered to your door. You can stream music, films, and TV shows. You can pay for goods and services when you don't have any cash on you. You can dictate notes and messages while you drive. You can control your central heating and other devices at home remotely. You can transfer money without going to a bank.

You get the picture. The list of clever things smartphones can do is almost endless, and growing all the time. All this, from one small device that can be obtained for a few hundred dollars.

What is happening here is a much more efficient use of resources. Going back right to the start of this chapter, we know that economics is simply the endeavor of making the best use of scarce resources. And technology does just that. The time savings alone from technological advances are staggering.

So if we are saving time and money through technological advances, it simply does not make sense that we continue to see inflation year after year. But that's what we have. Unsound fiat currencies have enabled governments to continue engineering inflation, despite massive deflationary pressures from technological progress.

Deflation is demonized by economists and central bankers the world over. It is continually framed as a phenomenon that must be avoided at all costs, something that would suffocate any economy that was unfortunate enough to cross paths with it. But as we know, economists don't always get everything right. So what would a deflationary economy actually look like?

Firstly, we should clarify here that neither bitcoin nor gold are deflationary currencies at present. The supply of both continues to increase each year, but at a very slow rate. Much much slower than the rate that fiat currencies are printed. And in the case of bitcoin, eventually, all bitcoin will be mined and at that point, the supply will cease to continue growing.

Given its slow rate of supply growth, bitcoin would most likely result in a deflationary economy if it was to be adopted as a global currency. What that means in practice is that each year your savings would be able to buy a little bit more, as your money would appreciate against the value of all goods and services produced.

Rather than the consumption-driven fiat economies of today, where it's almost a case of spend it or lose it, a deflationary environment encourages people to save for their future, and invest rather than spend.

This is simple mathematics. If you are earning a steady wage and prices of goods and services fall, you can afford more real things for every hour that you spend working. Consequently, you are becoming wealthier; your standard of living is improving. This would be true for the majority of society and is the opposite of what we see today, where you need a pay rise every year just to avoid becoming financially worse off.

Proponents of inflationary monetary policy will argue that deflation destroys productivity and results in significant job losses throughout economies. This may be true in the short-term but in a truly deflationary environment, this is simply not the case. In actual fact, what you would start to see is a *more* efficient allocation of resources.

Deflation encourages businesses to reduce borrowing

and maximize operational efficiency. Inefficient companies are more likely to go out of business and allow those resources to be re-deployed more effectively. This competitive environment encourages firms to be more innovative and continues to fuel advancement, as we have seen in the technology sector. Put all together, this improves standards of living further still.

What we have seen over the past century are cycles of inflationary periods followed by deflationary crashes. A good analogy is that of an alcoholic. The inflationary period is the drinking session, followed by a deflationary hangover. The booze is fiat currency. The economy gorges itself on cheap money, and swells as stocks and other assets start to form bubbles. Then it all comes crashing down and we go through a debilitating period of deflation.

This is partly why deflation has such a bad reputation, after all, who likes hangovers? Like them or not, however, they do serve a purpose, they are a message that we need to stop, a chance for the body to recover. Likewise, deflationary periods are a chance for the economy to reset, rid itself of deadwood and come back more efficient. The problem is, as the hangovers have got worse and worse over the years, the method used to deal with them has been to keep the booze flowing in ever larger quantities, through measures such as quantitative easing.

This might mask the problem for a while, but as we know, you can only go on drinking like this for so long before you encounter serious health problems and ultimately death.

So we have a structural problem here. The major emerging industry of our time, technology, is deflationary by nature, but we have those in charge determined to avoid deflation at all costs by inflating their way into oblivion. Why are those in charge so hell-bent on avoiding deflation at all costs? One word; debt.

As we have discussed, the global economy is absolutely riddled with debt. Leveraged up to the eyeballs. And what happens to debt during periods of deflation? Well, the value of money is increasing in real terms, so those debts are actually getting *more* expensive to repay. This is a significant problem when debt is at the highest level on record.

Even if a new deflationary world economy would ultimately benefit society, it is how we get there that is the real challenge. There is no obvious way that we can transition into this brave new world.

Economies could be allowed to collapse under the pressures from the ongoing global pandemic, but allowing businesses to fail is simply not palatable to politicians who are looking to be re-elected at some point in the next 4 years. The alternative is to try and inflate their way out of trouble, and ultimately end up bailing out almost everyone. This may work for so long but the level of money printing required to do so would almost inevitably lead to significant inflation, or possibly hyperinflation.

The idea of scrapping fiat currencies and returning to some sort of gold standard could provide a solution but again, it is very unlikely there would be political appetite for such a move, or international agreement on any such measure.

So what can be done? Well, there is one final option that might just be the solution we need. Yes, you guessed it. Bitcoin.

Bitcoin could be the sound money that we desperately need to transition onto for a better future. Most powerfully of all, if the people make that choice, and enough people start to adopt it, it could become a de facto global currency, over which no sovereign state would have control or the power to stop. Now there's a thought.

Just as Friedrich Hayek foresaw in 1984, governments will not give up monetary control easily.

But Bitcoin might just be that roundabout alternative that cannot be stopped.

The Why Chapter Summary

- Economics is all about scarcity; a problem of how to best use limited resources to meet as many needs as possible. Value is derived from supply and demand.

- The earliest form of economics was trade through barter; swapping goods and services so that all parties can utilize resources more effectively.

- Money was created as a medium of exchange. Something of common value that was widely accepted, to enable different types of goods and services to be exchanged more easily.

- Money has taken many different forms but up until the 1970s it centered around gold, first through gold coins, then by paper currencies pegged to the value of gold via the gold standard.

- Gold found itself in this position due to its high stock-to-flow ratio. It is a scarce, durable asset that holds value well, as new supply is a small fraction of total gold reserves.

- Money has always been susceptible to manipulation by governments through debasement, and episodes of hyperinflation have occurred in countries the world over.

- As of 1971, the US came off the gold standard for good, and currencies were then left "floating" against each other as fiat currencies not backed by an underlying asset.

- Fiat currencies have enabled governments to manipulate their own currency and fund their spending through excessive borrowing.

- Government deficits and national debt have ballooned and since the 2008 financial crisis, many governments have been engaging in quantitative easing, or money printing, to keep the credit bubble from bursting.

- Money printing benefits those at the top most, as they see the money first. The poor suffer a reduction in purchasing power whether any of the new money reaches them or not. Asset prices begin to form bubbles. Inequality increases.

- The current inflationary system is unsustainable but due to the structural nature of the problem, there is no easy solution.

- Benefits of bitcoin include greater accessibility for those without bank accounts and more secure custody due to its non-confiscatable nature.

- Adoption of bitcoin as a global currency would likely lead to a deflationary monetary environment which would benefit wider society and drive innovation.

- While governments will not relinquish control over the money supply easily, the decentralized nature of Bitcoin means there is very little they can do to stop it.

5. Why Not

"So, That's the End of Bitcoin Then"

- *Forbes, 2011*

We've now outlined the origins of Bitcoin, its functions, uses, and ultimate purpose. But you may still have some lingering confusion or doubts around certain aspects of the cryptocurrency.

Being a relatively new technology that is not governed by a central authority, it is very easy for misinformation to spread about Bitcoin and other cryptocurrencies. You may have seen the acronym "FUD" used; this stands for fear, uncertainty, and doubt. It is common to see FUD spread about Bitcoin in the mainstream media and elsewhere. Sometimes this is driven by a sheer lack of understanding of the technology and its implications, other times it can be a bit more malicious. Certainly, the banking sector and anyone heavily invested in it, may see Bitcoin as a threat and, therefore, they will not hesitate to publicly denounce it.

But the fact remains that despite all the negative publicity, Bitcoin has not died, imploded, crashed and burned or faded into obscurity. That's not to say it cannot fail, but it has overcome every challenge thrown its way to date. This chapter is designed to de-myth some of the FUD you will hear and to give an honest and balanced assessment of Bitcoin's capabilities and flaws.

Fact Or Fiction?

“Don’t waste your time with Bitcoin. This new coin is vastly superior. It can do X, Y, and Z and has real-world adoption!”

We are talking here about altcoins. An altcoin is any cryptocurrency other than Bitcoin. Some of the better-known ones that you may have heard of are Ethereum, Ripple (XRP), or Litecoin, but there are thousands. One of the most common traps that people fall into when they first research cryptocurrencies, is concluding that these altcoins are superior to Bitcoin. Usually, because they have a faster blockchain that can process more transactions per second or some other amazing new feature that Bitcoin simply cannot match.

This is partly true, many do have superior technology in terms of processing transactions quickly, however, virtually all of them suffer from the major drawback of having some form of centralized control. Being decentralized is exactly what makes Bitcoin unique and what makes it so precious as a store of value. To further negate this point, bitcoin can function perfectly well as a store of value without the need for rapid processing of transactions, and what’s more, the Lightning Network is now addressing that issue for small payments.

You will come across many altcoin fans online who will swear blind that their altcoin is the next big thing and a “Bitcoin killer”. They have most likely failed to grasp the monetary properties that make bitcoin superior.

Another trap that many people fall into, is investing in altcoins that cost a few cents per coin, believing that one day they might be worth $20,000 per coin like bitcoin as its peak. While theoretically possible, usually the reason these coins cost a few cents is that, unlike bitcoin, which has its supply capped at 21 million coins, many altcoins have a supply of billions and billions of coins. Therefore, for each one to increase in value to thousands of dollars it would require an unfeasibly large amount of money to flow into that cryptocurrency.

"Facebook is making a new Bitcoin so soon everyone will switch to that."

Facebook is indeed planning to launch its own cryptocurrency known as Libra. Let's be clear, it is not a new Bitcoin. It is nothing more than what's known as a stablecoin.

A stablecoin is a type of altcoin that is pegged to the value of an existing currency such as the US dollar. There are already several dollar-pegged stablecoins in existence and Libra will be another. Libra will have the advantage of being directly connected to billions of users through their Facebook accounts, however, any stablecoin linked to dollars has all the problems associated with fiat currencies that we discussed in the previous chapter. As a store of value, it will be no more useful than paper dollars and, therefore, in no way impinges on Bitcoin's viability. That's not to mention the potential privacy-related issues that a Facebook-owned cryptocurrency might bring.

Furthermore, Libra was originally planned to be pegged to a basket of different fiat currencies, but under pressure from authorities it has already yielded and agreed to only peg to one fiat currency per cryptocurrency. It is, therefore, no less susceptible to centralized control than the paper money printed by the central banks themselves.

"Bitcoin wastes huge amounts of electricity and is an environmental disaster."

There is no denying that the Bitcoin network consumes a significant amount of energy to keep operating, around 60 TWh per annum, and continuing to increase. That's equivalent to the annual electricity usage of a small developed nation such as Switzerland.

Bitcoin seems to have come under attack because this figure is so easily quantifiable and so vast. However, to assess whether that criticism is fair we must look at where this energy is coming from. The majority of bitcoin mining takes place in China, with the second most productive region being Sichuan. Sichuan is home to a number of overbuilt hydroelectric dams and actually has twice as much power as its electricity grid can support. It has, therefore, turned to bitcoin mining to monetize this excess energy that would otherwise be wasted.

The ease with which energy can be converted to cash through bitcoin mining, means it enables spare electricity that would otherwise be wasted to be utilized. Therefore, it is not true to say that all the electricity used mining bitcoin is generated specifically for that purpose. There are also many spurious claims around CO2 emissions that crudely extrapolate CO2 emissions from traditional methods of generating electricity. Again, much of the power used to mine bitcoin is generated from renewable sources such as hydro or solar, that would otherwise be surplus to requirements.

When assessing Bitcoin's energy consumption, we must also consider whether this energy is creating anything useful. A decentralized, trustless, censorship-resistant digital currency must be considered very useful by many people, as Bitcoin's adoption has continued to grow, and people are starting to recognize that it can solve some of the issues associated with fiat currencies.

It must also be considered alongside what is already accepted as legitimate uses of energy. Tonnes and tonnes of gold are mined every year, consuming massive amounts of energy, but this is not questioned. Big tech corporations use enormous amounts of electricity to power their servers, even if that is just for the purpose of consumers streaming another series. What's more, the fiat era has driven up energy consumption in uses which are more harmful for the environment, such as the production of single-use plastics.

When Bitcoin's energy usage is considered with all of the above in mind, the headline electricity consumption doesn't seem quite such a "disaster".

"Bitcoin is a scam."

Having read the previous chapters it should be evident that Bitcoin is not a scam. It is an open-source piece of software that is used by many people all around the world. There is no central authority in charge and no centralized holder or issuer of bitcoins.

The reason Bitcoin has been tarnished as a scam by many, is that con-artists and scammers do target its users as bitcoin transactions are effectively irreversible. There also tends to be a lot of confusion among many new adopters, which makes them particularly susceptible to scams. Unfortunately, like all other forms of payment, bitcoin is a target for fraud, however, used with effective security for your private keys, it is actually a much more secure way of transacting as there is no reliance on a trusted third party.

Bitcoin's reputation has also not been helped by the scores of copycat cryptocurrencies that have since been launched, many of which are under the control of developers with nefarious intentions to pump up the price before dumping their supply of coins on the market.

"Bitcoin is a Ponzi scheme."

A Ponzi scheme is a fraudulent investment scam, where early investors profit handsomely by drawing in more and more new people to invest. They will normally be dressed up as a legitimate business opportunity, where everyone benefits by convincing more people to invest. In reality, all that is happening is that earlier investors are using newer investors' funds to pay themselves a return. When the pool of potential new investors dries up, the scheme collapses and those that were late to the party lose their money.

It is nonsense to compare Bitcoin to a Ponzi scheme. It is true, that if more and more people invest in bitcoin, you would expect the price to keep rising due to the simple laws of supply and demand. However, this does not make it a Ponzi scheme. Any investor in bitcoin is holding a liquid asset that they can convert back to US dollars or another currency at any time. They are not reliant on new investors joining to get their money back. Like any investment, the value of bitcoin can go up or down and it is up to the individual to properly assess the potential risks and rewards involved.

"Bitcoin is used mainly by criminals and drug dealers."

This is another favorite spin of the mainstream media. It is undeniable that bitcoin is used by criminals. This fact is actually a testament to its success. It is a censorship-resistant decentralized currency that governments cannot seize, so of course, criminals will look to exploit this. While some may see this as a weakness, it is also bitcoin's biggest strength. The lack of a central authority to censor transactions, takes the control of money out of the hands of the state and puts it back in the hands of the people.

As we have seen, the current government-controlled system may be useful for freezing the assets of criminals, but where do you draw the line? It is also highly susceptible to corruption and has the potential to rob any ordinary citizen of their freedom. Just ask any person under the rule of a tyrant. Not to mention the plethora of problems that have been created by fiat currencies.

What's more, the idea that bitcoin is inherently bad because some bad actors choose to use it is severely misguided. Criminals also like to use dollars, smartphones, vehicles, real estate, and so on. You get the picture. None of these items are branded as the criminals' choice like bitcoin has been. If you were a criminal, do you think you would choose to use a currency where every single transaction ever made was recorded on a publicly available digital ledger? Or would you rather have a suitcase full of used untraceable paper banknotes?

"When governments see the threat Bitcoin poses to their control of the money supply they will simply shut it down."

This is understandably a genuine concern of many people. Governments will not relinquish their control of money easily, as it offers them access to the easiest money of all; fiat freshly printed out of thin air by central banks. However, Bitcoin has been moving quietly under the radar for some time and has now survived its first decade relatively unscathed.

The fact of the matter is, as Bitcoin exists only digitally, it is outside the jurisdiction of any one government. It also exists on a decentralized network of nodes, spread around the world in different countries. Therefore, no one country could possibly hope to shut it down on its own. Even if every government in the world tried to shut it down together, they would need to locate and destroy every node on the network; failure to do so would result in the network just starting up again. Given that a node can be run on a fairly basic computer with an internet connection, shutting them all down is simply an impossible task.

The area where governments could damage Bitcoin's progression is the infrastructure that surrounds the network, such as mining and exchanges. A ban on mining would be easier to enforce, although still virtually impossible to close down completely, and bans on exchanges could starve the network of the fiat on-ramps it needs to continue growing.

However, this is simply not what is happening. The US perhaps has the most to lose, if bitcoin was to take the US dollar's reserve currency status, however, they are actually one of the most open countries in embracing it. It has been classified as a commodity in the US since 2015 and there are now several bitcoin futures contracts traded on major exchanges, that make it accessible to institutional investors. The development of other cryptocurrencies, such as Facebook's Libra, should also actually improve fiat to bitcoin on-ramps, as millions of people will have access to cryptocurrency for the first time.

Previous bitcoin bans in China and India have now been repealed and it has been reported that many other countries are actively considering mining bitcoin with excess energy. This is perhaps not surprising as nation-states start to recognize the potential first-mover advantage in adopting bitcoin. Just ask any investor from the early 2010s and they will tell you, that it paid handsomely to get in early! Those nation-states that start accumulating bitcoin now stand to do very well should it ever become a global reserve currency.

"Bitcoin is always getting hacked."

It's not hard to see where this line of thought comes from. There have been countless examples over the years of people losing bitcoin due to exchange hacks. These events are often widely reported in the media and can trigger the bitcoin price to crash. The worst of these was the Mt. Gox incident in 2014 when 850,000 bitcoin were stolen.

While these events have been plentiful, it is worth noting what is actually happening here; hackers are targeting the weakest link in the system. It is not Bitcoin itself that is being hacked, it is the exchange which is holding users' bitcoin that is having its private keys exposed. The bitcoin are then just transferred out of the exchange's wallet into the hackers'. Therefore, this type of hack can very easily be avoided if you simply store your bitcoin in your own wallet and protect your private keys properly. Bitcoin stored in this way is virtually impossible to steal through hacking.

The Bitcoin network itself has a running uptime of 99.99%, meaning it is virtually never down. Even the best tech companies struggle to match this. Bitcoin can operate so successfully because it is decentralized on thousands of machines, meaning there is no single point of failure for hackers to target.

While exchange hacks were commonplace in the early days, the infrastructure is improving all the time and this is now much less of a problem than it used to be.

"It is only a matter of time before quantum computers can break the encryption that Bitcoin uses, rendering the network useless."

Quantum computers are the next generation of computers that are currently in development and promise processing power like never seen before. While Bitcoin's current 256-bit encryption requires significant computer power to crack, thus ensuring the security of the network through proof-of-work mining, it is believed that quantum computers could break this type of encryption much more quickly.

Any weakness in the encryption on which the entire network is based, could lead to massive security issues with Bitcoin. All confidence in the system would likely be lost and the value of bitcoin would collapse.

Quantum computing is not yet at a point where it could be used to steal or hack bitcoin, however, most experts believe that could become a reality sometime in the coming decades. While the threat may not be imminent, given the scale of the threat, it is already on the radar of many Bitcoin developers. And they're not the only ones. The entire internet, including online banking, is based around 256-bit encryption, so quantum computing will almost certainly lead to quantum-proof encryption also being developed.

To secure Bitcoin in a quantum world, the Bitcoin protocol would simply need to be upgraded with quantum-proof algorithms. Given the importance of this type of update, it can be safely assumed that there would be a wealth of developers working on this and the change would be adopted by all users without issue.

"Bitcoin has no intrinsic value. It isn't backed by anything."

This is a common criticism of Bitcoin that you will hear from proponents of the fiat system and many gold bugs, those that advocate a return to the gold standard.

The simple response to these people, is to ask what dollars and gold are backed by. They will no doubt respond by saying the government backs the dollar and gold has an intrinsic value because it is used in various forms of production.

Dollars first then, make no mistake about it, they are backed by nothing. Holding dollars does not entitle you to exchange them for anything at the bank. They are paper IOUs from your government and have no intrinsic value.

Now gold. Although gold does have some uses in production, does this really give it intrinsic value? What even really is intrinsic value? Isn't all value subjective? If humans suddenly decided they no longer wanted gold jewelry, surely gold's value would be impinged, even if we're led to believe that its value is intrinsic.

Gold is commonly held as a safe haven asset in times of economic turmoil. Why is it regarded in this way? Because everyone acknowledges this to be true, it is a self-fulfilling prophecy. The reason gold has evolved in this way is due to the characteristics that make it sound money; limited supply, high stock-to-flow, and highly durable. It does not trade at $1,700 per oz because that is its intrinsic value, it trades at that price because it was the hardest form of money we had yet uncovered.

Bitcoin is the same. You can argue it has no intrinsic value on the grounds that neither does gold. But it does have value. If enough people decide it is a hard form of money that they want to invest in, it is likely that that value will continue to increase. It is backed by a decentralized, censorship-resistant network and the will of the people to hold it.

"Bitcoin is just a bubble that burst. Now earlier investors are just trying to create hype to get their money back."

Bitcoin has indeed been through a number of bubbles that have subsequently burst. The parabolic uptrends known as "bull markets", have historically then given way to "bear markets" where the price crashes in the region of 80% from its peak. You could argue that the bitcoin bubble burst in 2012 and 2014, but each time the price has recovered and gone on to make new highs.

Many people struggle to understand Bitcoiners' resolve and their eternal desire to HODL. Bitcoin enthusiasts' passion for the cryptocurrency is not driven by a desire to get their money back, nor do they intend to introduce new people for this purpose. Bitcoiners understand the value Bitcoin has, due to its design and the important role it could play in resolving many of the issues with the current global fiat monetary system.

"Bitcoin is too volatile to be used as any sort of currency."

At the current stage of Bitcoin's development, this is true. As a currency, it is simply not practical with the wild price swings from week to week. What we must remember, is that Bitcoin is still a fledgling technology, something akin to email in the mid-eighties or the internet in the early nineties.

As Bitcoin develops, the extreme volatility should reduc, as the price begins to plateau once it has reached a certain level of investment. It is estimated that currently there are only around 25 million bitcoin users globally. This may sound like a lot, but it is much less than 1% of the world's population, meaning we are still well within the realm of early adopters. As infrastructure improves and adoption grows, the level of inflows into bitcoin will keep increasing and the volatility will eventually subside. It will still fluctuate relative to other currencies, but this is true of all currencies in use today.

"Bitcoin is too slow to ever be useful for making payments for millions of people."

The Bitcoin blockchain is limited in terms of transaction speed and the time taken to mine each block. For large payments and cross border payments, this is still an improvement on the current options offered by banks, which usually take several days to process. For smaller payments, it is a problem, but the Lightning Network should go a long way in resolving this issue by processing micropayments on a second layer atop the blockchain.

Even if other blockchains can process transactions much more quickly, the appeal of bitcoin as a store of value will remain. Think of it as the gold in the gold standard. Gold is hopeless when it comes to transacting due to its lack of portability, but it remained an effective basis for money for centuries, before the gold standard was eventually abandoned.

"Transaction costs with Bitcoin are really high."

This is another criticism that is often levied by proponents of other cryptocurrencies. Bitcoin transaction fees may be higher in some instances, when the network is very busy and clogged up. In these situations, transactions with higher fees get processed first, so if you're in a hurry to get your transaction through you may end up paying for the privilege. However, normally that would not be the case and you can attach whatever fee you are happy to pay. It could even be free. In addition, the Lightning Network promises extremely cheap or free transactions as they are performed off-chain.

What's more, compared to traditional banking, bitcoin transactions are still extremely cheap. Particularly for large payments, you can move significant sums of money with bitcoin for a few cents, where your bank would normally charge tens or even hundreds of dollars.

"Bitcoin is too complicated, why would I use it when I can pay for things much more easily with cash or a credit card?"

This is another issue resulting from where we currently are in Bitcoin's lifecycle. It is certainly tricky to grasp at the moment, for people who are not technically minded. Copying and pasting public keys to make a payment and keeping private keys secure, can be difficult for many people. Again, to use the example of the early days of the internet and email, this was not something that was user-friendly. Just trying to connect a machine up to the internet through dial-up took a bit of doing, and then it was so slow to load anything that many people didn't even bother with it. However, nowadays the internet is everywhere and it has become so user-friendly that even the least tech-savvy person probably has a smartphone in their pocket.

Bitcoin has the advantage that much of the required technological infrastructure is in place. It does however face one unique challenge and that is custody. People are just not used to holding their own assets. One of Bitcoin's biggest strengths is perhaps one of the biggest headwinds to adoption; there needs to be a significant improvement in the custody solutions available to end-users.

Ease of use will be a key area of development for Bitcoin in the coming years and with increased adoption, we will likely see rapid improvements in this area. For example, we are already starting to see wallets that can be run on smartphones and debit cards that can be linked to cryptocurrency wallets.

"Bitcoin has many high-profile critics and there's no smoke without fire. If it is such an amazing new technology, why are these people so unaccepting of it?"

Let's look at some of the most vociferous critics of Bitcoin. Warren Buffett is regarded as one of the world's greatest investors, yet he is repulsed by the idea of Bitcoin. In the past, he has labeled it a "delusion" and also once called it "rat poison squared". Surely then, if such a superstar investor wouldn't touch it with a barge pole, it must be a terrible investment?

Although Buffett may be a great investor, it is no secret that he has missed out on huge gains by not investing in technology stocks, and by his own admission, he says he doesn't invest in anything he doesn't understand.

Perhaps then, we can understand why he wouldn't necessarily want to invest, but why be so critical? One look at his fund's holdings might tell you, as his portfolio is heavily weighted towards banks. The very industry that Bitcoin threatens to disrupt.

Other notable critics include Bill Harris, the former CEO of Paypal, who outright labeled Bitcoin as a "scam" and Jamie Dimon, the CEO of US bank JP Morgan, who in 2017, called Bitcoin a "fraud". Do you see a theme developing here?

Many outwardly critical public figures have an ulterior motive, so it is always wise to take these criticisms with a pinch of salt. It is also telling that these criticisms often do not extend beyond calling Bitcoin a scam, fraud, or bubble, with little to no reasoning attached. There is plenty of great educational material about Bitcoin available online, so it is encouraged that you do your own research and reach your own conclusions, rather than listening to the talking heads on the television.

6. Conclusion

"It might make sense just to get some in case it catches on. If enough people think the same way, that becomes a self fulfilling prophecy."

- *Satoshi Nakamoto*

Take a breath. You're nearly there. You now know What, How, Why, and Why Not. Of course, this book is not exhaustive, it is designed just to give you an insight into Bitcoin. Each of the chapters in this book can be delved into in much more detail with further reading, and hopefully, you will now have some areas which have taken your interest that you'd like to learn more about.

As we've seen, Bitcoin is not as simple as *just* being a new technology, a new currency, or a new digital asset. Bitcoin was born in a financial crisis, and could perhaps solve the next. While it is formed of simple bits, it solves a complex problem that has stumped computer scientists for years. The concept is straightforward, but it has endless potential to revolutionize the lives of millions of people around the globe.

To fully understand this potential, Bitcoin must be

viewed through a multi-faceted lens, that shows not only its technical capabilities but also its potential as a financial tool for freedom. A glance through this lens opens up a bottomless rabbit hole of discovery, about the world around us and how our very own societies are being impacted by the financial control of the state. Bitcoin started life as a technology experiment but it is rapidly developing into a financial experiment that we can see playing out before our eyes.

Block By Block

Bitcoin started life as a technology experiment more than anything else, a brainchild of some cypherpunks perhaps. Bitcoin's early days were just a proof of concept phase. The main users were Satoshi and a handful of other miners. While the whole network was worth peanuts, this early usage was essential in ironing out issues with the code and proving that Bitcoin could actually work from a technology point of view.

It *was* possible to run a network over a decentralized base of machines. It *was* possible to hash blocks together in such a way that they formed an immutable digital ledger. It *was* possible to do all this even with basic hardware and limited internet speeds at the time.

Where many projects had failed, Bitcoin achieved success in garnering adoption. The main reason for this, was that it actually *worked.*

It didn't take long before the inherent usefulness of digital cash came to fruition. With wider awareness, Bitcoin entered a new phase, a phase where people were using it to make payments online. While the price may have been extremely volatile, the ability to send money over the internet without the need for a bank was too attractive for many to refuse.

It is no secret that a large number of these payments were for illicit purposes such as buying narcotics. Bitcoin also found use funding otherwise censored entities such as Wikileaks. This has contributed to a long-standing negative stigma around Bitcoin which many people still hold to this day. But while there were negative associations, the use of bitcoin in this way went a long way in confirming its viability as a means of payment.

Let's face it, if it *could* have been shut down by governments, it almost certainly would have been at this point. The very fact that lawmakers were powerless to stop it, just proved its concept further. While Bitcoin was demonized in the press, the additional attention more than likely helped its cause by increasing awareness of the cryptocurrency. As they say, there is no such thing as bad publicity!

And bad publicity is what Bitcoin has continued to receive. When the price goes down, it is declared dead, and when it goes up, it is proclaimed to be a scam or the bubble of all bubbles. The old guard is clearly feeling threatened by Bitcoin, you just have to look at the comments of any bank to see this. Beyond this, the level of unfounded negativity and misinformation around Bitcoin in the mainstream media is quite concerning.

Bitcoin tends to pop in and out of the public's consciousness, usually as the price rises and falls, and it is these hype cycles that continue to bring Bitcoin into more and more people's awareness. These people often aren't interested in buying narcotics over the internet, but what they are interested in, is making a profitable investment. You can call them speculators, or investors, or just your average guy on the street in many cases. Bitcoin's meteoric rise could not fail to attract those looking to make some money.

With this interest, Bitcoin moved from being purely a tool for making payments, to an investment instrument, albeit the most risky one the world has ever seen. But with great risk comes great reward, and the outrageous potential returns on offer continued to attract many, as Bitcoin moved from payment medium into a form of digital gold.

Investors were mainly retail at first, normal folks investing a few hundred or a few thousand dollars, but soon enough, large institutional investors, such as hedge funds, began to take an interest. In its current phase, Bitcoin is being prepared for institutional investment. Financial derivatives, such as futures contracts, have been launched and can now be accessed on some of the largest exchanges in the world. All the while, online cryptocurrency exchanges work tirelessly on improving infrastructure, to make cryptocurrencies as accessible as possible for as many people as possible.

Satoshi's small experiment, which initially whurred into life on a single machine, has now spread around the globe and amassed a network of thousands upon thousands of machines. It is worth hundreds of billions of dollars. But where does it go next?

The Future

When Satoshi created the genesis block with the immortal words "The Times 03/Jan/2009 Chancellor on brink of second bailout for banks", this was perhaps a sign of Bitcoin's intended ultimate purpose.

Bitcoin is constantly evolving and has been through a number of transitions already. Is it possible that it is now ready to embark on its greatest act yet? Is it ready to take up the mantel as the world's reserve currency and effectively end the fiat era?

It's impossible to say, but its chances have never been better. While the global debt mountain has been steadily rising unnoticed by many, over the last 50 years, we have now reached a tipping point. The ongoing global pandemic has brought that into razor-sharp focus, as we see central banks flooding economies with cash printed from thin air.

The general public is beginning to ask questions and you can understand why. They have been fed a delusion over many years that economies are fine because the stock markets are booming. Many now find themselves out of work, facing an uncertain future.

On a more granular level, people are starting to wonder just where all the money is coming from, to fund the stimulus checks and the furlough schemes. They are starting to question why they pay taxes at all when governments can seemingly produce money at the drop of a hat. The media continue to perpetuate the illusion that this money is borrowed and will be repaid. It is simply not true. Any sums that are repaid will most likely be paid for through additional borrowing, exacerbating the problem further.

Viable solutions for the situation we now find ourselves in, are in short supply. Bitcoin *could* be that solution. The road ahead may be rocky and it would certainly take some time, but the return to sound money that Bitcoin offers, could lead us into an exciting new world.

A new world where an honest day's work is fairly rewarded. A world where people can make a better future for themselves by saving and investing carefully. A world where nations work together collaboratively and conflict remains limited. A world where people are free to move their wealth with them, wherever they go. A world where corporations are required to create something truly valuable. A world where people can live freely without the fear of oppression, censorship, or tyranny.

You may think this is all a little bit fanciful. But the hard evidence is there. Money is intrinsically linked to every aspect of our lives. The monetary base used, can dramatically affect our standard of living. Just look at a country suffering from hyperinflation if you want to see an atrocious example of this.

You may also think it fanciful that Bitcoin could become a global reserve currency. Not so long ago Bitcoin didn't even exist. At first, they said it would never work, but then it did. Then they said it would be shut down, but it wasn't. Then they called it a bubble, but it reached new peaks time and time again. Then they said other cryptocurrencies would come along and kill it, but it lives. They said it has no intrinsic value and it will go to zero, but it hasn't.

Bitcoin doesn't care what *they* say. So long as the network is maintained, Bitcoin will continue churning out new block after new block, regardless of what is said about it, who uses it, or any other factor in its external environment. What Bitcoin does next depends on *us*.

As a society, if we choose to make it our new global monetary base, it is there, ready and waiting. Equally, if we choose to marginalize it, it won't go away completely, but it could be significantly stifled.

We are living in unprecedented times socially, economically, and environmentally. Change is coming whether we want it or not. Perhaps for the first time, we are truly empowered to make those changes for the better.

What happens next is up to you.

7. Additional Resources

If you want to learn more about Bitcoin there are loads of resources available. The following are some that are highly recommended:

Websites

Bitcoin.org

Bitcoin Wiki - https://en.bitcoin.it/

Books

Bitcoin: A Peer-to-Peer Electronic Cash System (The Bitcoin Whitepaper) - Satoshi Nakamoto

The Bitcoin Standard - Saifedean Ammous

The Growth Delusion - David Pilling

The Price of Tomorrow - Jeff Booth

The Little Bitcoin Book - Bitcoin Collective

Podcasts

Stephan Livera Podcast - Stephan Livera

Off The Chain - Anthony Pompliano

Tales from the Crypt - Marty Bent

Bitcoin Rapid-Fire - John Vallis

In addition to the above, you can find loads of great content online on Twitter.

8. Glossary

51% Attack - disruption to a blockchain caused by a miner, or group of miners, with over 50% of the network's mining power

Address - an identifier of 26-35 alphanumeric characters that represents a possible destination for a bitcoin payment

Altcoin - a cryptocurrency other than Bitcoin

Barter - a method of trading where goods or services are swapped, in the absence of money

Bear Market - a decline in market price over a period of time, generally accepted as a 20% decline over a two-month period

Bitcoin - refers to the Bitcoin entity or concept

bitcoin - refers to a quantity of coins, e.g. 10 bitcoin

Block - a collection of transaction data that is added to the blockchain when a miner solves the associated math puzzle

Block Reward - the payment a miner receives for adding a new block, consisting of transaction fees from the block added and a quantity of newly mined bitcoin

Blockchain - an immutable collection of all blocks

mined to date, maintained on a decentralized peer-to-peer network

Bond - a debt instrument issued by governments and companies; an agreement to repay the bondholder on a certain date with an agreed amount of interest

Bull Market - an increase in market price over a period of time, generally accepted as a move of 20% off the lows

Cantillon Effect - the theory that expansion in the money supply does not impact prices evenly; those nearest the source of new money benefit most

Central Bank - a national bank responsible for implementing monetary policy and regulation of member banks, with the power to issue new money

Crypto - shorthand for *cryptocurrency* or the cryptocurrency industry

Cryptocurrency - digital money that can be transferred without a third party via a decentralized peer-to-peer network

Cryptocurrency Exchange - a website that enables users to buy or sell cryptocurrencies with fiat currency

Cryptography - a method of protecting information through the use of codes so that only those for whom the information is intended can read and process it

Cypherpunk - an activist advocating the use of cryptography to ensure privacy and security

Debasement - the action of reducing the purchasing power of a currency through an increase in the money supply

Decentralized Network - a network hosted on multiple machines with no reliance on a central authority or server

Deflation - a reduction in the general level of prices in an economy

Difficulty Adjustment - the change in the complexity of the math puzzles in each block, updated after every 2,016 blocks mined

Digital Ledger - the collection of all transactions recorded on a blockchain

Economic Stimulus - a measure introduced by government or central banks designed to galvanize the economy

Encryption - the process of converting data or information into a code to ensure privacy

Fiat - a currency that is not tied to any underlying asset, backed only by government

FUD - fear, uncertainty, and doubt

Full Node - a computer or device that contains a full copy of the blockchain and verifies all rules of Bitcoin

Futures Contract - a financial instrument that obligates parties to transact an asset at a predetermined future date and price, commonly used by institutional investors

Gross Domestic Product (GDP) - the total value of goods produced and services provided in a country during one year

Halving or Halvening - when the quantity of newly created bitcoin in the block reward is reduced by 50%, occurring after every 210,000 blocks mined

Hash - a proposed solution to the block puzzle, generated by a miner

Hash Rate - the speed at which a miner can propose solutions to the block puzzle

HODL - hold on for dear life

Hyperinflation - rapid price increases in an economy, generally accepted as over 50% per month

Inflation - a general increase in prices in an economy and a subsequent reduction in purchasing power

Lightning Network - a payment protocol operating through a second layer atop the Bitcoin blockchain

Miner - a full node that also adds new blocks to the blockchain through the solving of the math puzzles within each block

Money Supply - the total face value in circulation of a given currency

Node - any computer that connects to the Bitcoin network

Peer-to-Peer (P2P) Network - a collection of computer systems connected via the internet that share files directly with each other, without the need of a central server

Private Key - a secret number enabling bitcoin to be spent from a wallet

Proof-of-Work - a system that requires a not-insignificant amount of effort to produce a piece of data; new blocks are created through resource-intensive mining

Proof-of-Stake - a system where new blocks are validated according to how many coins a user holds

Public Key - a number used to generate addresses to which bitcoin can be sent

Quantitative Easing - a monetary policy where a central bank purchases government-issued debt, in effect supplying the government with newly created money

Reserve Currency - a strong currency widely used in international trade, with the current global reserve currency being the US dollar

Satoshi or sat (unit) - the smallest denomination of bitcoin, equivalent to one hundred millionth of a bitcoin

Stablecoin - a cryptocurrency whose value is pegged to another currency, such as the US dollar

Trade Deficit - the amount by which the cost of a country's imports exceeds the value of its exports

Trade Surplus - the amount by which the value of a country's exports exceeds the cost of its imports

Wallet - a device, physical medium, program or service that stores private and public keys enabling bitcoin to be stored or spent

Whitepaper - a document issued to promote or highlight the features of a solution, product, or service.

Zombie Company - a corporation that needs bailouts to

operate or an indebted company that can repay interest on its debt but is unable to pay down the loan principal

9. Thank You

Finally, I'd like to thank you for reading this book and I really do hope you have found it useful.

If you have enjoyed this book, it would mean a huge amount if you could pass it on by leaving an honest review on Amazon. I feel it is an important subject matter and it would be great to help more people learn about it.

You can also reach out and find me on Twitter; *@BitNoi*

Made in the USA
Middletown, DE
14 November 2020

24062287R00106